THE MAIL

Ships

◦◦ NOVELLA TWO ◦◦

NAOMI FINLEY

Cover designer: Victoria Cooper Art
Website: www.facebook.com/VictoriaCooperArt

Editor: Scripta Word Services
Website: scripta-word-services.com

READING ORDER FOR SERIES

Novels:
A Slave of the Shadows: Book One
A Guardian of Slaves: Book Two
A Whisper of War: Book Three (Coming Soon)

Novellas:
The Black Knight's Tune: Novella One
The Master of Ships: Novella Two
The Promise Between Us: Novella Three
The Fair Magnolia: Novella Four

Novels can be read alone or with the novella series.
The author's shorter works are best read in the suggested
order.

Prologue

Charles
London, 1832

I COULDN'T DRINK IT AWAY. THE IMAGE I'D CONTRIVED OF MY wife in my brother's arms seemed to reside permanently in my mind. I drained my mug of ale and slammed it down on the counter.

"Another?" asked the tavern owner, his sometimes thick, sometimes sparse brows drawn low, hooding his eyes.

I waved him away. Squinting from the throbbing pain in my head, I rubbed the sides of my temples.

"How about you come upstairs with me?" whispered a woman, her hot, ale-laced breath dampening my ear.

I glowered over my shoulder at the blond tavern wench with intense blue eyes. "I think not." My jaw tightened with disregard.

"A handsome feller like you ain't meant to spend the evenin' alone." She pulled her lip between her teeth and pressed her body against me.

"I assure you, if I wanted to bed a woman, which I do not, it wouldn't be a tavern whore."

My intended bite seemed only to entice her more. Her fingers trailed up my inner thigh, and I cringed at her touch.

"Why so angry?" She poked the simmering rage, long established, inside of me.

"I suggest you remove your hand, or you'll wish you never set eyes on me this evening."

Unaffected by my threat, the brash woman moved to stand in front of me, inches from my face, her breasts spilling over the top of her green calico dress. The warmth of her body pressing against my knee conjured a low rumble in my throat, and the desire for human touch stirred within me.

For a brief second, I wanted nothing more than to ease the ache hollowing out my chest. The endless supply of ale had scarcely taken the edge off. *To bed this wench would block it all out...* For a few minutes, at least. Then it'd all come rushing back. Guilt. Pain. Rage. The taunting images.

"No!" I pushed to my feet, threw some coins on the counter, and strode to the door.

"Ain't right in the head, that one." The woman's voice trailed after me.

Outside, the cool summer breeze chilled the sweat beading on my forehead. Resting my forehead on the stone wall of the tavern, I tuned in to the agitating sounds of merriment drifting out from inside. Two men stood next to me, watching me. Through blurred eyes, my brain foggy from drink, I boldly returned their stare.

"Shall we relieve you of your fine attire?" said the thickset man in a patched brown coat, worn thin from years of wear.

I straightened and stepped back from the wall. I felt my lip curl as heat invaded my belly. "If you desire to lose a hand, then by all means, I invite you to try."

"You threatening us, mister?" The thinner of the two squared his shoulders, his fingers flexing at his sides. The duo crept forward, smiles of triumph already centered on their faces.

If the men had come looking for a fight, gentleman or not, I'd send them crying to their wives like the little boys they were. The trip across the Atlantic Ocean had not eased what festered inside me. I clenched my hands into fists and raised them to chin level, ready to take on my attackers. "Take it how you like, but I warn you, turn away, or you will regret—"

"You heard the bloke. Now off with you, before we make fish food of your hides and they find you belly-up in the Thames," a man's voice with a heavy Irish accent warned from the shadows of the building.

"Who's saying?" the burly man said, whirling around to search the night. "Show yourself, you bloody coward."

There was a grumble accompanied by a curse, then a copper-haired man stepped into the light seeping from the surrounding homes and establishments. I'd expected a man of towering stature to emerge, but the man was of average height and hardly intimidating at first glance. If one were observant, which these men were not, one would note the hard set to the stranger's face—this was a man one thought twice about before speaking back. "Name's Gillies."

"Irish scum, I see." The slighter man spat on the ground. "What's it to you, what we do to the rich American?"

"I don't much like blokes that attack a man when he's down."

"Can't handle his drink, is all." The bulky one rested his hands on his thick waistline. His hands disappeared within the folds of fat.

"Maybe so, but if you're not wanting to meet my friends waiting in the alley over there," Gillies nodded across the street, "I suggest you go on your way or return inside for another drink."

The men eyed each other, called the man's bluff, and advanced on him. I heard the crack of fists landing on flesh. Cries echoed down the alley, and a series of curses. It was all a blur in my current state. My brain told me to move my feet and aid the Gillies fellow, but my body stayed rooted in place. I shook my head to clear the muddle of intoxication.

"Come on, let's get out of here," a man cried, and the pounding of feet echoed on the cobblestones.

"Keep it quiet down there!" a woman bellowed from an upstairs window across the street.

"Might do you well to hail a carriage." The Irish accent informed me of the victor of the brawl. My defender raised two fingers to wipe away the blood dripping from the gash across the bridge of his nose.

"I'll be fine. The fresh air will clear my head."

"Have it your way, then. I won't be around to save your hide next time," he said.

Heat burned my neck and ears. On any other day, I'd be appalled that a man half my stature had come to my rescue. What little common sense I had left found me. "Thank you, Mr.—"

He bowed his head. "Gillies. Hugh Gillies."

"Yes, well, much obliged."

"Be warned, American—the streets are dangerous at night, and in your condition…deadly."

I tipped my hat, and without another word, turned and walked down the narrow street toward my townhouse. The path in front of me seemed to weave as I tottered onward.

Beggars of all ages huddled in the corners and on steps of establishments. Rats scurried in the gutters, nibbling at the trash lining the streets. My stomach roiled at the over-powering stench of sewage. *Maybe I should've hired a carriage…* "No, the air will do me good," I said, and pressed on, ignoring the logic clamoring in my head.

I veered into the alley leading to the glowing lights of the main street. My thoughts shifted to my wife and her newborn daughter back at Livingston, and my pulse beat faster.

In the early days before we were married, when Ben came home from medical school, we would visit Livingston, and while I got caught up in business obligations with Olivia's father, I'd hear Ben and Olivia laughing as they strolled the grounds. Her father had taken a liking to me, and I'd admired his business smarts and aspired to be like him. While trying to hang onto every word of wisdom he bestowed on me, I watched them through the window with harmless envy. Never once did I give much thought to their relationship beyond the friendship we all shared.

When Ben returned to school, I had more opportunities to converse with Olivia without the distraction of my brother on my visits to Livingston. However, our talks somehow centered on him; I suppose it was our shared affection for him. Our friendship warded off the loneliness of weeks and months spent at sea. I'd daydream of seeing her again and hearing her laughter, and sometimes my fantasies would swell with a stolen kiss. When I docked in Charleston, her face was the one I longed to see first. I'd ride to Livingston and she'd greet me with genuine happiness.

Her father's failing health pushed him to seek a husband for his daughter and he'd chosen me, much to her dismay. In a blink I found myself wed to Olivia and months later we found out she was with child. When Olivia and my brother had come to me with the news that the unborn child my wife carried was not mine but his, it had been like a kick to the gut. The momentary bewilderment soon turned to seething rage. I'd demanded they remove themselves from my sight, and swore never to speak to them again. Although they claimed their abstinence after Olivia and I had married, I couldn't look past her love for my younger brother. I tried. Oh, how I tried. I'd been a fool not to notice she'd fallen for him. How could I have been so blind? The perpetual torment from the question never eased. After their revelation, I had ruled Livingston like a tyrant, unable to conceal my anguish.

Beauty such as hers had caused many men to fall. Guilt had pummeled me at the ill-appointed thought. Olivia was no temptress; she'd been a young girl in love. But the betrayal I felt over the love she held for my brother had guided my actions the day Olivia, swollen with pregnancy, had gone missing in the swamps, only to arrive the next morning, dirty, her skirt torn, to deliver the news that Ben had rescued her. She deflected my questioning about the slave trader's claim that a pregnant woman had aided a runaway child.

I still wondered where my brother had disappeared to after his knightly rescue. Would he always be the hero in my wife's world? To my knowledge they had adhered to the bargain we struck when he finally arrived back at Livingston later that evening. We all agreed I would raise the child with Olivia on one condition: that Ben remove himself from our lives.

Then came the day my wife's screams of childbirth echoed through the house. I'd hesitantly gone to her bed-side, where Olivia sat propped against the headboard, surrounded by pillows. Henrietta perched on the edge of the bed and they stared in awe at the infant in my wife's arms. Tears of happiness flowed freely over Olivia's supple cheeks, and the undying love radiating from her face as she'd looked down at the cap of dark curls, the pink mouth, and alert eyes of the infant had awakened all the emotions of betrayal I'd fought to bury. As I peered down at my niece, I'd swallowed back the fear swelling in my chest. Fear of the bond Ben and Olivia would always have.

"Charles," Olivia had said, reaching for my hand, her face glowing with joy. "Isn't she beautiful?"

I pulled back my hand and stared at the child, long and hard, before looking at my wife. Her chestnut hair flowed over the shoulders of her white cotton night-gown—never had she been more beautiful. That day she held her daughter and studied me with pain-filled eyes. Her lips parted as if she wanted to say something, then a firm determination set her jaw and darkened her eyes before she looked away. She looked down at the babe and ran a hand over her head. I'd recognized her protectiveness, as I'd seen it in mothers before. A tear slid from her eye.

I turned on my heels and marched off. After instructing Henrietta to pack my trunk, I went to tell the groomsman to prepare the carriage. I set sail for London late that afternoon, never returning to say goodbye to my wife, or to look upon the child.

A month later and an ocean apart, my heart ached, stoked with each memory of her. With each couple I passed, I wondered if, with my abrupt departure, my brother had returned. Did he even now hold my wife entangled in a passionate embrace? Were their days spent relishing the happiness of the child's birth?

Such torment had turned me to a nightly indulgence of liquor, consumed until I collapsed into bed, senseless and vacant of emotion, only for sleep to plunge me into a fitful night of dreaming.

As I moved on in the direction of my townhouse, I forced all thoughts of home from my mind. I focused on the alley ahead, becoming aware of a dark form blocking my path. Throwing a look back the way I'd come, I calculated the distance. It was shorter to continue. I cautiously walked on. *Probably someone succumbed to drink.* As I drew nearer, I noticed the small bare feet of a child or woman sticking out from under a gray cloak. Suddenly attuned to the sounds around me I scanned my surroundings, half expecting an ambush.

"You sick?" I nudged the form with my foot.

No reply.

I cast another glance around before peering down at the lump at my feet. Cursing under my breath, I squatted, balancing on my heels, and gave the person a gentle shake. Wetness coated my fingers. I lifted my hand and held it close to my face. Blood.

My heart sped up, and my alertness peaked. Pulling back the dark hood of the cloak, I sucked back a sharp breath.

A woman.

Warm breath brushed the fingers I placed to her mouth. She was alive but appeared to be unconscious. I rose to my feet and wiped a hand over my face. Hands on my waist, I paced. *I can't just leave her here in the street.*

"Why didn't I hire a carriage?" I grumbled. Once more I knelt beside the still form, and shuffled her into my arms. Under her weight, with the ale making flimsy puppet strings out of my muscles, I staggered to my feet. Trudging through the alley, I willed myself to stay upright. I had no intention of becoming a victim to the gangs who roamed the streets.

As I stepped out into the glow of the streetlights, relief shot through me. I whistled to hail a carriage and half climbed, half stumbled up the carriage's steps with my human bundle. I deposited her on the seat across from me before ducking my head out and giving the driver my address. I sank into my seat, breathless, as the carriage lurched forward.

The hood of the cape had fallen back, and in the dim lights from the street, I regarded the woman. Long lashes brushed her dark cheeks. Her full mouth was pressed tight in a grimace.

The carriage stopped outside my townhouse ten minutes later. I shuffled the woman into my arms and disembarked. I paid the driver and stood in the street until the carriage pulled away and disappeared into the fog and amber glow of the streetlights. I turned and walked up the steps to the front door and banged on the door with my foot.

Moments later, my groggy English butler, Julius, answered in his nightclothes. "Mr. Hendricks." He gawked at the bundle in my arms. "W-what do you have there?"

I adjusted the woman in my arms. "I found her in the alley."

"B-but w-why did you bring her here?"

I looked from him to the woman. Why had I brought her here? I didn't rightfully know. "She's hurt. Send for the doctor. We'll see to it that she's mended and send her on her way." I pushed my way inside.

"B-but sir," the man protested. "A w-woman in your home? And a Negro. It w-won't look good."

A Negro? I regarded the woman. Yes, I suppose Negro blood ran in her veins. The urgency and reasoning in Julius's words struck me. *Fool!* I chastised myself. Wishing for the night to be over, wanting only the solitude of the darkness of my chambers, I said, "I'm aware what others will think. That's why you won't say a word. You'll pay the doctor a handsome sum to keep him quiet. Now get dressed and fetch the doctor."

"Yes, sir." He bowed and ambled off to his quarters at the back of the house.

I carried the woman down the corridor to the guest chamber and kicked the door open. I walked to the bed, carefully laid her down, and stepped back. A low moan came from her. I stared at her in the dim light from the full moon, which trickled across the floor into the lantern-lit corridor, illuminating her face. Though the woman bore Negro blood, it didn't seem to be the only blood coursing through her.

I lit the lantern on the bedside table, then moved to the basin on the stand under the window. I caught my reflection in the glass as I poured water into the bowl. My hair hung long and unkempt, and thickening whiskers shadowed my usually clean-shaven face. I splashed it with tepid water, the shock of it energizing me before I lifted a cloth, wiped my face, and returned to the bedside.

I undid the button fastening the woman's cloak at the base of her throat and inspected her injuries. There were bruises under her left eye and along her throat, those marks resembling fingerprints, as though someone had clutched her neck. Was she a freed black? Or had she taken the silk cloak from her mistress? The cloth wasn't something a slave would own. If she'd fled, that would mean someone was looking for her. Or maybe someone had tired of her rebellion and disposed of her in the alley. Only a fool too rich to grieve the loss of property would do such a thing.

Leaning over her, I pulled back the cloak and examined her back. She winced and mumbled something inaudible. My jaw tightened at the sight of the lashes that pulverized her back. The whip had eaten away the fabric of her simple gingham dress and splayed her flesh.

Mud caking her feet from the streets led me to believe the woman had fled. Finding the woman here would cast suspicion on me and affect my business dealings in London.

I lowered myself onto the edge of the bed. Her eyes fluttered and opened. I jerked in surprise. "Hello."

Her eyes widened in terror, and she dug her heels into the bed and struggled to get away from me, her efforts drawing a pain-filled cry.

"I won't hurt you." I lifted a hand to calm her. "I've sent for the doctor to attend to your wounds."

"No!" she gasped.

"If we don't treat your wounds, they'll get infected."

A fierceness entered her green eyes, and I swallowed the thickening in my throat. Olivia's face filled my thoughts, and I pressed her image away and rose. The woman scampered up against the headboard, drawing up her knees, pain tugging at her face.

I took a few steps back. "You've nothing to fear. I'll tell no one you're here. If you're running from someone and they were to find you here, it'd mean harm to both of us. You can rest and heal, and then you must go."

What had I been thinking of, bringing her here? I hadn't. I pulled my fingers through my hair. My need to drown my sorrows in excessive drink had landed me in this predicament.

She cocked her head and uncertainty flickered in her eyes. "No doctor," she said. "I know how to tend my wounds."

"Are you sure?"

"It isn't the first time I've suffered this fate." Emptiness echoed in her voice. That emptiness prompted a surge of pain in my soul. Suddenly the room felt like the walls were closing in on me. My heart raced, and my breathing became restricted. I strode to the door.

"Who are you?" her soft voice trailed after me.

Without turning, my hand clutching the doorjamb, I said, "Charles Hendricks...and you?"

"Isabella."

❧ CHAPTER ❧
One

Charles
London, 1841

T HE MASTS OF THE *OLIVIA II* CRACKED AND SNAPPED IN the late-morning wind. Above, gulls soared, squawking and beating their wings as the bow of the ship parted the waters of the harbor and thrust us toward the congested Port of London. Small fishing boats bounced and swayed in the swell of our arrival. Soon the cesspool of London and all its glory stretched out before us.

With *Olivia II* moored at the wharf along the River Thames, I left the captain to deal with the inspection by the customs officers and made my way to Thames Street to hail a hansom cab. With a bellow from the driver and the crack of a whip, the cab lurched forward, and I braced a hand against the wall to steady myself, grumbling under my breath at the impatient driver.

The carriage threaded through the crowded streets toward Charles Hendricks & Co., the tailor shop I'd opened at Olivia's insistence. My weakness when it came to my wife had allowed her to dabble in the affairs of men. But she'd had an exquisite eye for clothing and thought it'd be a wise investment. And how right she'd been. We'd acquired the wealthiest clients in London and its surrounding areas.

Six dark, meaningless years had passed since she was taken from us. My guts twisted with the memory of her limp body, blue and dangling from the rope. I'd held her body in my arms, bathing her face in my tears, and promised to find the bastards responsible. Yet I'd failed to deliver on that promise and each year it ground away at me. Her murderers roamed free while I struggled to go on.

The open sea had become my refuge from the estate that had entombed me. Each day the dead spirit of my departed wife haunted me. The hallways of Livingston whispered her name. Reminders of her had seeped from every corner of the estate—the curtains in the parlor she'd had designed after seeing a similar set in a hotel during our wedding journey in France. The settee she'd had me bring all the way from Thailand for the drawing room. And the most significant reminder—my daughter.

Seasons had yielded my heart to the child, and I'd come to love her. But she'd become a painful remembrance of what we'd both lost. Some days I envied my nine-year-old's young mind and how it had dissolved all recollection of her mother. Shame charged through me. Had I not played a part in that?

I had wronged the child. Grief over Olivia's death and my failure to protect her had driven me to remove all traces of her from the mansion and the property. Workers and slaves who'd known Olivia had been sold or moved off to my other estates. Only a few trusted slaves remained.

Had it not been for the attachment and love Willow held for her mammy, the debt I owed the woman and the night that bound us together, she too would've been sent away. My daughter's jagged weeping, along with Henrietta's plea of "Please, Masa, don't separate me from de li'l miss. She already lost so much", had been the final factor in her staying on at Livingston. In return, we'd agreed Olivia's name would be banned—it became the only way I could find peace in life. The only way I kept myself from going mad. Try as I might, it hadn't stopped the racing of my heart when I caught a glimpse of a dark-haired woman in a crowd or witnessed the fire of insubordination in my daughter's eyes.

Nights at sea, when I couldn't sleep, I'd stroll the deck and my mind would trick me into seeing her. Like a phantom, a goddess of the sea, she glided across the ocean, a vision in white billowing fabric, her eyes smiling with the affection I liked to believe she held for me in the end. A cry would rumble in my chest before it parted my lips with her name. What I wouldn't give to embrace her one last time and feel the warmth of her body next to mine. To explore the tenderness of her kiss on my lips. I'd tell her I was sorry for the blinding rage I'd held toward her and my brother. I'd take back all the horrible things I'd said—words breathed that could never be undone. *May God forgive me.*

"Get out of the bloody way!" shouted the driver.

I pulled back the black velvet curtain to peer outside as the buggy swerved down the last street en route to Charles Hendricks & Co. I was just in time to see a hungry, dirty-faced street urchin leap to the side to avoid being pulverized beneath the horses' hooves. I banged on the roof of the carriage with a fist. "Slow down, you fool!" Releasing the curtain, I leaned back in the seat, pressing two fingers to my eyes to ease my exhaustion.

London had a way of capturing my thoughts and launching them into another season in life. A time that seemed like a century ago.

The face of another woman came to mind.

Isabella…

After the apprenticeship system was abolished in '38, Isabella had disappeared without a trace. She'd told Mrs. Dier, the head dressmaker at Charles Hendricks & Co., to thank me for purchasing her from her previous master. I had my suspicions that the Dutch woman knew more about Isabella's whereabouts than she let on. Over the years, she'd remained tight-lipped when I'd inquired about Isabella but, not one to be deterred, I had continued to try.

The carriage pulled up outside the shop, the driver opened the door, and I made my exit. "Do wait; this won't take long," I said. The driver nodded.

I marched toward the door then, thinking better of it, I spun on my heel. "It'd serve you well to drive with care," I said gruffly.

His face contorted in the most unbecoming expression and he thrust out his hand. "Pay me my fee, and you can find another driver."

Biting back a reply, I reached inside my coat for my pocketbook. After retrieving sufficient payment, I thumped it against his chest. He grabbed it, waved a hand in irritation, and climbed aboard the carriage seat. Spitting a curse and then a series of derogatory remarks, he cracked the reins and the carriage charged off.

"Mongrel!" I muttered. Rubbing a hand over the nape of my neck I squared my shoulders, strode up to the door, and seized the handle.

Inside, a clerk behind the counter spoke with a woman dressed in yards of silver silk. He looked up and smiled at me before continuing with their transaction.

Everything from velvets, silks, and taffetas to the most exquisite lace and ribbons imported from around the world lined the walls. Women and girls ambled throughout the shop, stroking and cooing over the ceiling-to-floor shelves of fabric bolts. Gentlemen waited in the wings, somewhat bored, or eyeing the merchandise with the same admiration as their womenfolk.

Olivia's words came back to me: *"If one wishes to outsell the competition, it's essential to present excellent goods and employ the most skilled dressmakers and tailors available."*

"Mr. Hendricks, I wasn't expecting you," Mrs. Dier said as she parted the dark blue damask curtains separating the back room and stepped out.

My palms dampened with anticipation as, not to be dissuaded, I strode toward the hunchbacked woman. Time had capped her blond hair in a net of silver and had taken its toll on her health, but the intensity of her eyes revealed she was still mentally spry.

"Yes, I just arrived. I thought I'd come by and check on things here before I headed home to freshen up after the long voyage."

Her keen gray-blue eyes narrowed. "And to inquire on Isabella?"

Heat burrowed through me. "Have you heard from her?"

"No," she said, her eyes shifting to the front of the store. Mrs. Dier withheld the truth from me, I was sure of it.

I took her by the elbow and led her into the back room. Her body tensed under my fingers. "I suggest you unhand me, Mr. Hendricks."

My jaw tightened at her defiance. "I should've thrown you out on the street long ago at your disregard for who employs you."

"The same threat you've spewed the last three years." She shook her elbow free. She was never one to bow or cower to a customer, or me, for that matter. Though I wanted to send her on her way, the business had thrived because of her dedication, talent, and a firm hand with the customers. All things she was well aware of and cleverly held over me as leverage. Blast the woman!

"I must see her."

"I told you, I don't know where she is. And if I did, I wouldn't tell you. Isabella's no longer enslaved to you."

"You know she was more than that—"

"Oh, I'm very aware she was more than that to you. You wooed the poor woman into your bed," she said through clenched teeth.

"Mrs. Dier! I warn you to watch your tongue," I said sharply, then lowered my voice. "She was...she *is* more than that to me."

"I urge you to leave her be. You and I both know, as does Isabella, that you don't love her—"

"I care about her."

Her pale face reddened and she scoffed. "She deserves more than your pity and attempts to take care of her financially. Negro blood may pump through her veins—" With a warning glare from me, she lowered her voice as well. "She's as fine a lady as all the highfalutin sows that come in here."

"You know what you imply can never be." My reply came out more like the hissing of a cottonmouth.

"So *she* says." She crossed her arms over her sagging bosom. She glanced away, but not before I saw the tears dampening her eyes. I'd often thought the good Lord had left the cavity where her heart should be vacant, but the woman held affections for Isabella; I'd witnessed the way she'd nestled her under her wing like a stray starving kitten. Admiration fluttered in my chest for the abrupt widow. Had she not stood between me and what I sought, I may have allowed the warmth to simmer on a moment or two longer, but as she continued the warmth fluttered and faded. The invisible wisp of gray smoke floated toward the ceiling, taking with it my tolerance.

"For some reason," she said, "the girl holds you in high regard, as though one mention of your love affair would ruin you."

"It would."

"You used the girl, Mr. Hendricks. And I won't be any part in helping you to continue. I don't know where she is." Determination puckered her lips. That exact set of her mouth had carved years of tiny, threadlike grooves into the flesh around her thin burgundy lips.

I knew I'd get no further with the woman. "Have it your way, but rest assured, I will find her." I glared at her before pivoting to leave the wretched woman in my shadow.

She grabbed my arm, panic apparent in her voice. "Why must you disrupt her life? Leave her be."

I turned back. "Because I have to set things right. I know she cares for me—"

"You're a fool, then." Her eyes flashed. "Isabella has moved on."

I swallowed hard. "Moved on?"

"She's to be married at the end of the month," she said smugly.

"You old bat! You lie!" I grabbed her shoulders and felt her frailty under my grip. She winced; I released her and stepped back. Ashamed at my behavior, I opened my mouth to offer an apology but she stopped me with a retort.

"I assure you, I do not." She leveled hard eyes on me. I stared deep into them, searching, and reading the fear registered there—not fear of me, but fear of what my showing up in Isabella's life may mean for her.

Regardless of her concern, I needed to speak to Isabella and I'd hunt all of London to unearth her. I'd make right the mistake of the past. A lifetime spent loving someone whose heart would always belong to another was a fate I didn't wish on her—a future with no promise of love, bound to a person unable to move on. No. She deserved so much more. Though my heart would never grant me leave to love another as I had my wife, it still troubled me, abandoning Isabella the way I had: naked in my bed, her eyes so full of love. Fear had engulfed me and, like a coward, I'd ran.

CHAPTER
Two

Isabella

THE BEAUTY OF AUTUMN STRETCHED ACROSS THE countryside in glorious shades of orange and yellow. Fallen leaves whirled around my ankles and skipped across the front yard of the small cottage I rented.

Chickens clucked and bobbed their heads as they circled at my feet, waiting for their morning feeding. I scooped the feed into my apron and walked around the yard, raining food for my impatient customers. Behind me in the pasture, Moos-a-lot, our dairy cow, grunted her protest at not yet being tended to.

"Patience, old girl," I said, smiling to myself.

The sound of an approaching carriage drew my eyes to the lane. "I wonder who that could be at this time of day." I shielded my eyes from the bright sun to view the lane. I had no scheduled customers. Though with the Ainsworths' banquet only weeks away, I wouldn't put it past the persistent attendees to come calling without an invite.

I emptied the rest of the feed onto the ground and

went to wait at the pathway leading to the front door of the cottage. I smoothed back the flyaways escaping my thick plait and ran my hands over my gray woolen frock. Hardly a dress fit for guests. I fashioned gowns fit for Queen Victoria herself, yet I owned two frocks: one I received customers in and the drab one I wore.

The carriage came to a stop in front of me, and the footman jumped down and went to open the door. A bonnet trimmed in navy velvet poked out, followed by the flounces of a matching skirt.

"Isabella, I do hope you will forgive me showing up uninvited, but there's a matter I must speak to you about," Mrs. Dier said as her feet touched the ground.

"I hope it isn't anything to worry about, with you traveling out here so early on a Saturday morn."

The tightness in her timeworn face told me that something of grave concern had indeed brought her to my doorstep this day.

"You can take the horses around back and water them," I said to the footman. He nodded and boarded the carriage and the driver drove the team away.

I turned to Mrs. Dier and kissed one of her cheeks and then the other. "Shall we go inside and you can tell me what brings you here?"

Mrs. Dier's sparse brows arched. "Why, Isabella, I must say Miss Philippa's doing an excellent job with your lessons. Your manners and speech are of the utmost refinement."

I grasped at the compliment and tucked it away. Praise coming from Mrs. Dier was a rare and treasured occurrence. I offered an exalted curtsy. "If I must serve the ladies and lords of London, I must prove that I am somewhat refined."

"It is true; you must outsmart and outshine the prestigious ones if you wish to be endured. Beat them at their own game by rising in society. But you need not change for anyone. The 'country seamstress' has earned herself a name around the streets of London." She winked and bowed awkwardly.

I stifled a giggle. She was ever the sight, with her stooped posture and craggy facial features; add a cane, and Mrs. Dier would resemble a witch from the beloved stories I wove. And to think eight years ago I'd considered her unapproachable, with her unsmiling features and sharp tongue. As thorny as she was at first, I'd managed to insert myself into her small, suffocating world and tear down her barriers.

"It was under your tutelage that I learned how to fashion clothing that the aristocrats of London would consider worthy of purchase. And with this, most will look past the shade of my skin to obtain my garments."

"And such a pretty shade of skin it is." She cupped my cheek, and I absorbed the affection and warmth of her hand. Her eyes regarded me with earnestness, and I cherished the kindness Mrs. Dier had found fitting to bestow on me.

"Come." I slipped my hand into the curve of her elbow and led her down the stone path to the cottage.

The cramped cottage contained one main room that housed the kitchen and our seating area. In the back were two bedchambers, one I'd turned into a storefront to meet with clients. A path led from the front yard to a side door into the room. The room's large window overlooked the small garden and provided the best view and light. Some clients turned their nose up at our humble home but, as Mrs. Dier had said, they'd come regardless because they wanted my work. My designs had kept us sheltered, and though food was scarce at times, for the most part, we didn't go hungry.

I gestured for Mrs. Dier to take a seat on the bench at the small wooden table in front of the hearth. From a shelf, I removed two teacups with a pattern of gold leaves around the rim. One of the cups had a chip but, if you handed it to a guest handle first, it usually went unnoticed. I'd purchased them at the market, a splurge we surely couldn't afford but Pippa, the young woman who shared the cottage with me, had said if I hoped to convey the impression that I was civilized, there was no better place to start than to offer a cup of tea. However, most of my clientele refused to drink the tea for fear of contamination.

As we waited for the tea to steep, I lowered myself onto the bench across from Mrs. Dier and looked at her with curiosity.

She sat with her hands folded in her lap. "Well…" she said "…I'm not sure how to say this, but I had a visitor yesterday."

I waited for her to continue.

She registered troubled eyes on me. "Mr. Hendricks is in town."

My breathing caught, and a tremble rippled through me. "How do you know?"

"He stopped by the store."

"But why?" I said, immediately realizing the irony in my question.

She sputtered and arched a brow. "Besides the fact he owns the place? He came seeking you."

"You didn't tell him anything, did you?" My chest pounded.

"Certainly not!" Her eyes narrowed. "Though I question your choice to keep quiet, I understand your reasoning."

"He can't know. I fear what may happen—"

The door to the bedchamber creaked open, and we turned as Pippa and my five-year-old daughter stepped into the room. With a gentle push of her hand, Pippa guided Callie to stand before Mrs. Dier.

Callie curtsied. "How do you do, Mrs. Dier," she said in a manner fitting a lady of noble birth. Pride stirred in my chest.

"As fine as one can expect, Miss Callie." Mrs. Dier smiled. "Let me see if I can find anything for you in this satchel," she said, and opened her carpetbag to peer inside. "Ah, yes, just the item for a fine lady such as yourself." She withdrew a yellow silk dress embellished with lace cuffs and hem.

Callie squealed, clasping her hands together.

"Do you like it?" Mrs. Dier held it up for her inspection.

Callie bobbed her head, her eyes as large as old Moos-a-lot's. Mrs. Dier handed her the dress, and she pressed it to herself and twirled around the room. Pippa cleared her throat, and Callie stopped her spinning in mid-circle and said, "Thank you, Mrs. Dier." She shot a look at Pippa for her approval, who smiled tenderly at the child and nodded, securing a pleased smile from Callie.

"You're welcome, Callie love." Mrs. Dier had lost her husband before coming to London and never spoke of extended family. I'd often thought it a shame, with the grandmotherly affection she held for my daughter.

"Mummy!" Callie bounced over to the table and flung her arms around my waist. She peered up at me with pleading green eyes. "Pippa says that we can go in to town today."

I kissed the top of Callie's head and looked from Pippa to Mrs. Dier. "Today may not be a good idea."

Callie pulled back, her brow furrowed and her mouth turned into a full-out pout. "But why?"

"We'll discuss it later. Why don't you and Pippa go milk Moos-a-lot, so Mrs. Dier and I can hear over her bellowing to be fed and milked."

"Come, let's do as your mother asks." Pippa placed a hand on Callie's back.

Over the head of Mrs. Dier, Pippa's and my eyes met, and I nodded my thanks. She smiled and guided Callie toward the door.

Pippa and I were an odd pairing. She was the youngest daughter of Lord Buxton, disowned after she'd run off with a stable boy she claimed to be her one true love. Later he'd died in the cholera outbreak of '32. Too prideful to return home—not that his lordship would have accepted her—she'd become homeless, and I'd run across her begging on the streets.

Pippa gathered her shawl and Callie's from the peg on the wall by the door and, after they were bundled up, she opened the door, sending a gust of leaves and dust across the floor. They stepped out and closed the door, and I turned my focus back to Mrs. Dier.

"You are a clever girl, making Pippa the child's godmother. She truly cares for the child."

"Callie has blossomed under her care."

Mrs. Dier's lips parted then closed. Her eyes drifted back to the window.

"What is it? Speak what's on your mind." I poured the hot liquid into our cups. The aroma of bergamot citrus fruit permeated the air and slightly eased the tension behind my breast.

"The girl's learning quickly, and I think it was wise to have Pippa teach her the ways of a lady. It gives the girl a chance in society. But something tells me there's more to your asking Pippa to school her."

Nothing slipped by Mrs. Dier unnoticed. "She's a Hendricks by blood, and if by chance in the future something were to happen to me, I hope that…maybe her father wouldn't turn her away."

"Perhaps the reason you should tell him that he has a daughter to begin with."

"What? For him to reject her? No!" I shook my head. "I won't allow him to hurt her. You know he's a slave owner in America. And to have a daughter of Negro blood would…well, it'd ruin him."

"So your concern doesn't only run for Callie, but for him. You're still in love with him."

I shrugged and avoided a reply.

"You know he'll never marry you."

"I know." I bit my lower lip to quell its quivering.

My understanding of this exact knowledge had become clear after I had awakened in Charles's bed to find him gone. I'd been informed by his groom that he'd set sail to America and had left instructions that, when I awoke, his groom was to see me out. I'd gathered my things, and he'd shown me to the back door that led into the alley with the hope I'd go unnoticed. As though I were a slave summoned to my master's bed in secret, I'd slipped into the night.

A few months later I'd found out I was with child. And on Charles's return the following summer, I had already given birth to Callie. When he had stopped by the shop, I'd been in the back room. At the sound of his voice, I'd panicked. Retrieving Callie from the drawer she slept in, I'd thrown my cape around us and slipped out the side door and melded into the press of people and carriages.

"Oh, pet." Mrs. Dier slid her hands across the table, capturing mine. "How I wish you'd find a man that could love you in return. Someone to settle down with that would be a good father for the child."

"What man would want to raise another's child?"

"A good man."

"And Charles is not such a man?"

I envisioned the dark-haired child that'd entered the tailor shop with Charles and his wife that one summer of

'35. The child, I'd come to know, was the daughter of his brother and wife. Scarcely three at the time, she'd had a vocabulary beyond her years. She'd bounced about the shop with her small hand pressed in Charles's. She truly was a pretty child. I recalled how her happy chatter had echoed throughout the shop and how patrons stopped to observe her with admiration. And how she squealed with delight when Charles swung her up in his strong arms. "Oh, Papa." She'd flung her arms around his neck and squeezed with all her might. Then the beauty with emerald green eyes I identified as his beloved Olivia had drawn close and affectionately caressed the child's roseate cheek before bestowing a tender smile on Charles, who returned her gaze with one worshipping and overflowing with love.

At the time I'd been a senseless servant girl who'd fallen for her master—and a married man, at that. Although I'd never expressed my love for him until after his wife passed, guilt and shame burned within me each time I reflected on the growing fondness I'd borne for him back then.

Mrs. Dier's gentle grip on my hand pulled me back to the present. "Mr. Hendricks is a fine man, but he's a businessman first. An American that's neck deep in the slave trade. A man that's blinded by the color of your skin and will never see you for the woman you are."

I knew she was right yet, after all these years, the truth pained me. I suppose I'd always love Charles, but what Mrs. Dier hadn't realized was that not only my parentage kept his love from me, but the wife he'd lost. The woman who had stamped her mark on his heart, and in her death had taken it with her and left him empty and guarded.

There was a time I'd foolishly thought…maybe he'd have a small corner for me, that he'd learn to live without the woman deemed the fairest amongst women. But I'd soon learned there would never be space for another in his heart except her and the child she'd left behind. The child he'd signed on to become guardian and father to—greatness such as this lay within the flawed man behind the shell Charles offered the world.

Charles and I had made a ghastly mistake, the night we broke the threshold of friendship and succumbed to the pleasures of the flesh. A choice we'd made in the heat of passion. His desire to forget his deceased wife and my longing to be held by a man I'd fallen carelessly in love with had given me the most beautiful blessing in my life. My gaze turned to the window overlooking the yard, where Callie stood on the fence, stroking the cow's snout while Pippa sat on a stool milking.

Every time I looked into my daughter's face, I thought of him. Every time she narrowed her eyes in displeasure as he did, my chest tightened. The choice I'd made all those years ago not to tell him I was with child had been the right decision. I had learned to move on for my sake and that of my child, pushing the love I held for her father into the place I blocked from my thoughts. The place too scarred and damaged to venture into, the box inside of me where I stored the pain of missing my mother, the cruelty at my master's hands, and the hurt inflicted on me in a world where I questioned where I belonged.

Something fractured inside of me, pulling at the tangle of vines barring the vulnerable place inside me. Dampness strange to me formed in the corners of my eyes, and I dropped my head. Mrs. Dier stood, rounded the table, and gathered me in a gentle embrace. "There, there, love; don't be wasting no tears on a man." She stroked the top of my head. Her grumbling and ill words toward Charles didn't go unheard.

～ CHAPTER ～
Three

Charles

O UTSIDE MY OFFICE OVERLOOKING THE THAMES, THE skies grumbled and snapped as the rain that had started last evening continued through the gloomy drag of the morning and into the late afternoon. The fog simmered and stewed like a witch's brew as it crept from the river and swallowed up the docks and surrounding buildings.

"See to it that the shipment of tea that came in from India is on today's shipment to Liverpool. And the silk brocade needs to be stored properly and the orders fulfilled by the end of tomorrow. With the upcoming event at the Ainsworths' estate, the tailors' brows are starting to glisten with anticipation," I said to the lanky foreman who stood puddling the walnut floor of my office.

"Yes, sir. Right away, sir." He held his breath, awaiting my next command. His feet shuffled on the floor, his nervousness seeping through the room like a disease.

"Well, be off with you," I said with a vague wave of my hand. He scrambled toward the door like he was late for his next meal. "Oh, and make sure"—he froze at the sound of my voice—"Mrs. Dier's order is fulfilled first."

"Yes, Mr. Hendricks." His voice hitched, and he barreled out the door, gasping as the fresh air hit him, not from the cold of the dreadful weather, but because it was his first full breath since entering my office.

He'd no sooner left when an assertive knock rattled the door. "What is it now?" I said, stilling the movement of my quill on the parchment. My sour mood had hardly lightened after my arrival yesterday—Mrs. Dier had seen to that.

The door opened, and a russet-haired man with muttonchops stepped into the room. Not recognizing him to be employed by me, I stared at him through slit eyes. "Can I help you?" If constant disturbance was the forecast for the day, I'd never get any work done.

"Good day." He removed his water-stained tan hat and held it in front of him in steadfast hands, in direct contrast to the disquiet of my employee who had just fled.

"Well, get on with it, I've work to do."

"I've come seeking a job."

"A job? I'm fully staffed and don't require anyone at the moment." I waved a hand of dismissal and turned my attention back to the ledger in front of me.

But the man wasn't so easily dismissed. He inched forward. "Mister, if you'll only hear me out."

I looked at him. "Can't you see I'm buried in paperwork that needs my immediate attention?"

"Aye, sir, but this will only take a moment of your time, and I'll be on my way."

"Out with it, then, and make it quick." I removed my pocket watch and flicked it open. Half past three. I had a meeting with my banker within the hour. I'd never finish my tallies in time and make it halfway across London for the appointment, with the current rate of events.

"I'm one of the finest captains around these parts," he said. He tipped his chin up and arched back his shoulders. "I know the Atlantic to the Indian Ocean and clear to the Caribbean Sea better than any captain you'll find."

I studied the bold man. "Says who?"

"I do." His stance widened, and his striking blue eyes held mine. "I can handle a ship like no other man in all of London."

My curiosity building, I regarded him with assessing eyes. "Go on."

"I take pride in my work, and when I operate a ship the crew toes the line and my cargo arrives promptly without damage."

"Is this so?" I said. "Then tell me, Captain: Why are you here?"

"Well, I find myself in need of a job." His ruddy flesh deepened half a shade, but his gaze remained unrelenting. There was a familiarity about the man that made me think I knew him, which I was sure I did not. Maybe it was his average face and the fact that London was swarming with Irish and other immigrants.

I leaned back in my chair and smirked. "But you're the greatest captain in all of London. Yet you find yourself without a job."

His mouth twitched at my remark. "That's true.

But the reasoning behind my dismissal ain't what you think—"

"So you're telling me what I think now?"

"I'm telling you I was wrongly let go."

My teeth gritted with mounting impatience. "I'm giving you two more minutes of my time, so I suggest you make it worth it."

He nodded. "My name is Hugh Gillies…"

Gillies. Why did that name sound familiar?

"My previous employer was Earl Crawford."

I stiffened at the mention of the name. *Squalid, cheating bastard!* E. Crawford & Son had become a constant toothache. "I know the man," I said. "What did you do, that he dismissed you?"

"I refused to be part of his illegal transactions."

"Do be clear with your accusations, Captain Gillies."

"He has taken to smuggling Negroes, Irish, and poor alike into Brazil and America."

"For what purpose?"

"Why, to be sold as slaves and indentured servants." A fire flared in his eyes.

I studied the man. "And why should I care what he does with his ships? Furthermore, why do you?"

"Because making a profit off the misfortunes of others don't sit right with me. You see, I haven't laid eyes on my mam and da since I was a wee boy. They left for America with a seven-year term as indentured servants. Left me with my ailing grandma. They'd be creeping up on seventy or more by now—that's if they still draw breath." His voice cracked, and he dropped his head.

"Pardon me." He harrumphed and stared at the wall behind me.

I was aware of the illegal transactions of indenturing servants and smuggling slaves into America that still occurred. Law or no law, some men would continually endeavor to make a profit wherever they could.

"What do you want from me?" I said. "You're aware that I own slaves. Some of my crew on my ships are Negro slaves."

"Aye, but word has it, if there's a master to be owned by, you aren't the worst there is. Better yet, you ain't victimizing the street folk to thicken your pocketbook. Seeing as I find myself in need of employment, I'm figuring you got to be a smidgen better than Crawford."

I steepled my fingers against my chin. I wasn't in need of another captain. But to burn Earl Crawford would give me great pleasure, and with that I employed the cocky Captain Gillies.

❧ CHAPTER ❧
Four

Isabella

"YOU MUST WORK AROUND THE CLOCK TO ENSURE I have this gown for the Ainsworths' ball. Someone of your pedigree may not understand the importance of an event such as this, but I'm sure you've heard it's the event of the year. Gentlemen of the finest upbringing and financial security travel from far and wide with the hopes of securing a wife."

Standing on the pedestal in the middle of the room, the curvy, auburn-haired woman looked at herself in the floor-length looking glass. Her freckled hands pinching at her fleshy waistline, she continued to make faces in the mirror, sucking in her chubby cheeks to give the appearance of sculpted cheekbones. No corset possessed enough magic to conceal the overindulgence of cakes and pastries that had expanded her middle.

Pins clasped between my teeth, I mumbled, "I'll do my best."

"Your best simply won't do. Around the clock, I tell you. I must outshine that prudish Lady Clara. Word has it her father is losing his fortune and they aim to sink their hooks into the American tycoon, Mr. Hendricks."

My heart thumped faster at the mention of Charles.

"Can you believe Mr. Hendricks would be so blinded by her beauty?" she said. "Can't see the swine for what she really is. Besides, he's over half her age, but that doesn't seem to matter to the Ainsworths. Say, didn't you work as a dressmaker at Mr. Hendricks's tailor shop?"

"Yes, under the tutelage of Mrs. Dier." I tucked and pulled on the fabric before securing it with a pin.

"I can't see it being wise to step out on your own. With your lack of station and all, not to mention being an unwed woman atop of it." She shook her head, her lips pressing thin with disapproval.

I scurried around on my knees to fold the hem of the burgundy taffeta gown. Mention of my parentage had become as dull to me as if someone were inquiring on the weather—an almost daily occurrence. On the rare occasion I had passed as a white woman with my buttermilk complexion and my green eyes, most, after a torturous examination, categorized me as a darkie or of mixed blood—subhuman to the elite of London.

My ma had been a proud woman from the Caribbean. When she was thirteen, her parents arranged a marriage between her and the eldest son of a family in her village. The morning of their ceremony, Englishmen had raided their village, and my mother was seized from her hut and marched to a ship that waited offshore. *"Like the mouth of the serpent, waiting to swallow us whole,"* she'd said. *"Only to puke us out on this land plagued with sickness, hunger, and hate."* Enslaved in a strange country, my ma learned hatred was a way to survive; it made her feel something. She'd loathed every breath she inhaled of the stench-infused London air. *"There is no God in this place,"* she'd whispered into my hair one night as we lay in bed.

In her eighteenth year, she met my father when he came to deliver supplies to the home where she served as a chambermaid to the lady of the estate. One morning she'd stood on the balcony overlooking the front drive, beating the dust from a rug, when his wagon pulled up. He'd jumped down and taken off his hat before wiping the sweat from his brow. The sun's rays had bounced off his honey-blond curls. He'd caught sight of her shadow stretching over the ground, and peered up at the balcony where she stood. Her hands had ceased their movement. His steel blue eyes had been more beautiful than anything she had ever seen, but it had been what he'd done next that won her over—he smiled, placed his hat to his chest, and bowed.

After that day, when he'd show up for a delivery, Ma would meet him in the barn. Not long after, she became pregnant with me. For the first time she forgot how her heart longed for the motherland and what she'd lost. Pa was eight years her senior, but it hadn't mattered; they were in love. When her master discovered her pregnancy he threatened that, upon my birth, he'd sell me. Ma had fallen to her knees and gripped his hands, begging him not to take me—promising she'd do anything he asked of her.

My father was banned from coming to the estate and Ma saw him no more. But one of the gardeners said he'd observed a fair-haired man pacing outside the gate throughout the years, until one day he stopped coming. In my fifteenth year my mother died from scarlet fever, and I understood for the first time how empty and lonely life had been for her and how dark life would become for me. It was after her death, in the night after the household slept, that I came to realize what bargain she'd made with our master in her desperation to hold onto the one thing she had in life—me. And in her death I became the bargain, yet there was no bargain left to be fulfilled.

After Charles had purchased me from my master (how he'd succeeded, he'd never told me), I went in search of my father. The man at the livery where he worked said he'd died of consumption, but his wife said she believed he died of a broken heart. The husband had scoffed and accused her of romanticizing the facts. My father died never knowing of my existence.

"Isabella!" my customer whined.

"Forgive me; what were you saying?"

"You're sure to have the gown finished and delivered by tomorrow, right?"

"I'll deliver it myself."

"Splendid." Her smug, upturned nose poked toward the rafters. "I must be going. Papa's taking me to see Charles Kean perform Macbeth."

Once she was out of the gown and dressed in her own, I showed her to the door and stood in the doorway until the carriage disappeared down the drive.

"Was that the awful Manning woman?" Pippa rounded the corner of the house with a basket half full of apples from the nearby orchard.

"The one and only." I took one of the overripe apples and sank my teeth into it, leaning against the doorframe.

She adjusted the basket on her hip and settled her indigo blue eyes on me. "I do not miss a life of putting up with girls like her."

"Not in the least? Surely you miss the comforts your father's home provided? This life," I waved a hand around the property, "wasn't meant for a lady. Those clothes cover the backs of servants and the poor." I referenced her muslin dress, grayed with age.

In her father's house her flesh would not be marred by the elements, nor her nails blackened by the chores of a country girl. Her skin, darkened by the harshness of our lives, had not dulled her loveliness. Where my features were plain and unremarkable, she'd been endowed with beauty. Her blond curls were pulled back in a single plait; wisps had escaped her straw hat and brushed her cheeks in the afternoon breeze rustling across the fields. She was petite and perhaps a tad underweight, but her eyes gleamed with strange contentment at this ordinary life we shared. She'd become my dearest friend, and being without her seemed unbearable. I'd come to rely on her, perhaps too much, in assisting with Callie and around the homestead. She'd trained Callie and me in the ways of a lady and, in return, we taught her survival.

"The fanciest of cloth and treasures, or a household filled with servants to tend to your every need does not make a person happy." Conviction flared in her eyes before a distant sadness displaced the fire and a tender smile set on her pretty mouth. "Loving William, even if our time was too short, and living here with you and Callie, has brought me an abundance of happiness."

"But...don't you think of them?"

She looked past me in the direction of London. "I'd be lying if I said I didn't. I miss my brother and my sister. But my parents?" She fell silent. "Perhaps I miss what I wish they *could* be," she finally said, her voice heavy. Her chest rose and fell before her smile returned. "You taught me what true love between a child and a parent is, and with that I've come to understand what is—will be. I've realized that unless I walk in their shadows and mold myself into what society expects of a woman or what my parents want me to be, they'll never fully accept me. And one has to be all right with that if they're to move past the pain of rejection."

I stood, wordless, mesmerized by her resolve.

"Now, enough talk of things we can't change," she said briskly. "I know you've been putting it off, but we must go in to town. Or we'll starve, and poor Mrs. Dier will be left to tend to our funeral arrangements. Besides, it's Tuesday, and I know how you enjoy the market."

I had become observant to Pippa's will to exist in the moment and not be weighed down with things we have no control over, and I owed her for helping me find peace within myself from the past. Weeks had passed since Mrs. Dier had come with the news that Charles had returned and I'd stayed clear of town since. I knew paranoia fostered my hesitation because in a place as vast as London, blending in amongst the crowds would be easy enough. "Very well. Let me change, and we'll get ready for town."

"No need to change. You look smashing in that frock." She gestured to the cornflower blue calico I wore. I peered down at the dress. Yes, it was quite lovely, trimmed with beautiful scraps of lace and ribbons from Mrs. Dier.

"I do love this dress, but the luxury of wearing it other than to greet customers is one we can't afford," I said.

"Work, work, work. Life doesn't always have to be so serious, Isabella. There are days when you simply must let yourself breathe and enjoy the beauty of the day."

I looked at her a moment. There'd been a short period during my time with Charles when I'd glimpsed the world she spoke of, before it muddied with the reality of my lot in life. I didn't have time to daydream; we had to survive, and to survive we needed to eat.

"Maybe a little time away would be all right," I said, and turned and went inside.

CHAPTER
Five

Charles

BARROW AND DONKEY CARTS LINED EVERY CURB AND corner of Covent Garden. Street vendors sold an array of goods, from clothing to pies and puddings, crumpets, and kitchen drippings. The area once occupied by London's genteel now housed coffeehouses, taverns, and brothels tucked amongst other establishments.

Inside the market hall, I located the butcher's stall and pushed my way through the hordes of insufferable beings clogging the building. They pawed at the vegetables and fruit with germ-infested hands, their excited chatter speckling the produce with droplets of salvia. I cringed. They crammed into the aisles and, as if in a frenzy, pushed their way through, pressing against me from every angle. Faster and faster my heart raced as I considered the madness of my decision in coming.

The portly butcher rubbed his hands on his blood-spotted apron. "Mr. Hendricks, what can I do for you on this fine Tuesday afternoon?"

"My cook has sent me in search of your best slab of mutton for tomorrow's meal." I eyed the various cuts of beef and mutton hanging from ropes spiked to a wooden post.

His bushy brows beetled. "Gents like yourself usually send their cooks or grooms to fetch their household needs. But no one from your household has come to purchase from me except for yourself."

Where *did* my cook purchase the meat in my absence? I suppose I didn't rightfully know.

I feigned an interest in a leg of lamb far too generous for my household. "Do you oppose?"

"I merely wonder why, is all."

Wonder away, I grumbled inwardly, but said, "I prefer to purchase only the best cut of meat for my table."

As if forming a truce he held up his hands, the nail beds crusted with dried blood. "Have it your way, then. Take a gander and see what's to your liking."

I motioned to the shoulder cut I was sure would please the cook. My mouth moistened as I envisioned the delectable lamb roasted in a sauce of thyme and claret.

The butcher removed it from the post and held it out for my inspection. I inclined my head, and he turned away to wrap the meat in linen cloth.

While I waited, I turned to gaze over the masses of patrons, reflecting on the reason I found an excuse to visit the market in the first place. Isabella had said once that going to the market for her mistress was an escape. And over the years I'd often come to search for her, hoping to see her face amidst the market-goers passing by the stall I waited at now. She and the butcher had a friendlier acquaintance. She'd purchased from him for her previous mistress, before I'd rescued her from a terrible fate at her master's hands. Rescued her? After all, that's what I'd done—saved her from a master who had slithered down to her bedchamber, a closet under the stairs, long after his wife lay asleep, and demanded from Isabella his rights as a master.

The horrors she'd suffered at the hands of her master roiled my stomach and knotted my hands. During our night together, I'd kissed the burns left by the cigar he'd pressed into her body, and the ugly raised welts from the whip that over time had left her hazelnut flesh blanched. Our lovemaking had been tender and slow at first, until she had locked her fingers in my hair and captured my waist with her legs. Her eyes had grasped mine, and her hips had thrust with desire. The vulnerability she'd incited in me that night was paralyzing.

My thoughts drifted to a time when life had drowned me in a sea of panic and fear—the day charred into my memory; the day I'd found Olivia and the slave hanging by the river. Images I couldn't unsee chased me around like shadows of doom.

All night I'd searched for her, my torch but a glint in the blackness. I couldn't go home. Not while knowing she was out there somewhere, scared or hurt. Never had I experienced panic like I had as I roamed every trail and road looking for her. But all the worry of what could have happened hadn't prepared me for what I stumbled upon.

Pearls of sweat beaded my brow and a tremor convulsed through me, launching me back to a day I struggled to block from my memories.

෨෴ඁ

My eyes burn with weariness as I guide my horse down the trail that leads to the river. The feeling of dread that's settled in my stomach since Olivia's disappearance magnifies. A sense of knowing settles over me, daunting and paralyzing. The trees clear and the river comes into view. I scan the water for bodies, then the riverbank, and then in my peripheral vision I see them. Their lifeless, naked bodies dangle on ropes from the limb of a live oak.

"No!" my piercing scream echoes. I leap from my horse and pull the knife from its sheath at my waist. God! No! My feet pound the earth but seem to gain no traction. My heart thrashes hard against my ribcage. I reach the tree and cut through the rope suspending my wife. The line breaks and I dart to catch her body as it drops. Weak with grief, my knees buckle and I'm on the ground. My fingers tear at the white cloth marred with blood that's tied around her neck. It releases and through the dampness blurring my vision I read the words scripted with blood: Nigger Lover.

Confusion has no space in my mind. I toss the cloth to the side and brush back the hair escaping her combs to cover her face. Dirt smudges her cheeks, a bruise shines darkly on one cheek, and the flesh of her lip is split. My hand slips down to clasp hers, and I see the dirt caked under her nails—some broken in her struggle to escape. Pain breaks through my chest and a wail thunders through the afternoon.

"Olivia!"

Moments pass and I sit unmoving, lost in my grief. I open my eyes and stare numbly at the woman who had become the air I breathed. My reason for living. I'd spent our years together trying to measure up to the man she loved and the man I knew I could never be.

I lean down and kiss her cheek. "I'll find them," I whisper. "If it is the last thing I do with my miserable life, I will find them." My shoulders shake with sobs that shed no more tears.

Drained of emotion, I stand and lay her body down, then fetch a blanket from my horse and spread it on the ground. Lifting Olivia's body, I gently lay her on the blanket and wrap it around her.

I walk to the tree and cut down the slave girl. When her body drops into my arms, I know her fate outweighed the harm that came to my wife. A rumble vibrates in my chest, and my rage heightens. Laying her on the ground, I remove my coat and wrap her torso to conceal the mangled body beneath.

"They will pay! God help me...they will pay." My voice breaks.

A noise behind me sends me leaping to my feet. A colored man steps from the tall grass; fear visible in his face, his eyes flit around as he approaches.

"Who are you?" I say, my hand going for the knife at my waist.

He holds up his hands. "She your wife?" He motions to the blanket wrapping Olivia's body.

Feeling weak and helpless, I can only nod.

Grief ripples across his face. "Dis here be my fault," he says. "De missus was helping us."

I try to process his words. "Who?"

He turns and lifts a hand, motioning to the underbrush behind him. A Negro woman rises, and the grass sways and shakes *as she advances. She steps out and behind her trails a boy, a child but four or five years of age.* "Dis is my daughter and grandson. Your missus and her slave was helping us git to de next station."

The slave girl wasn't one of mine. I'd never seen her before. What was Olivia's connection to her? "What station?" I mumble.

His Adam's apple throbs as he swallows hard, as though he knows he has said too much.

"What station!" I bellow, and the woman clutches the child closer. I lower my voice, squeezing my trembling hands into fists at my side as I try to calm the rage overtaking the pain ripping through my chest. "Please…I must know who did this."

"White men. We heard dem comin' and de missus made us hide, here in de grass. She told us she'd be fine. But Ellie refused to leave her alone," he said. "Dey moved away so de men wouldn't see us hidin'. Soon as I heard dem I knowed they were drunk. But I never thought…I thought dey'd never touch a white woman. But out here wid no one to see… Dey never touched her de way dey did de girl."

"How many of them were there?"

"Three men and a boy."

Bile bubbles in my throat. "What did they look like?"

"I only got a glimpse of dem. One older man. Two younger." He hung his head. "I wanted…I had to protect my daughter from de same fate as Ellie." He nudges his head at the slave girl. "We all be daid ef we had moved."

"Why didn't you run off? I could blame you for this!"

"I knowed et. But I figured someone would come luking for de missus and dey deserved to know what happened to her."

"In what direction did they ride off?"

"Dat way." He points.

⌒⌒⌒

"Sir!" A grip on my shoulder pulled me back to the market with its murmuring crowd. I fought to regain my composure, to retreat behind the veil of reticence I'd built. No one could know of the weakness that consumed me. I rolled back my shoulders and released the air compressing my lungs. The deadness inside of me returned.

I looked to the butcher's hand on my shoulder, and he quickly dropped it. "You all right?" He coughed and stepped back, eyeing me with confusion.

"Yes, thank you." I collected the parcel he held in his other hand and shoved the money at him.

I departed the market hall, weaving through the costermongers, flower girls, and porters. Perspiration dampened my underclothing, and the urge to bolt became smothering.

Then a familiar face caught my attention. I glared at the man dressed in afternoon wear, and an animal-like noise rumbled in my throat. *Crawford.* Not in the mood for an altercation, I pivoted on my heel to meld into the crowd.

"Hendricks, is that you?" Crawford's voice boomed.

I cringed and halted. Dammit! Arching a brow at the sky, I mumbled, "Must you?" Squeezing my eyes shut, I craned my neck side to side to release the building tension and spun around to face him. "What finds you here in the middle of the day?" I said, eyeing the thin young brunette woman who stood with her gloved hand tucked in his elbow. Her resemblance to the man was uncanny, and she had the same hawkish gaze that traveled with unnerving thoroughness, as if she were two steps ahead of the current conversation, and plotting how she would outsmart you. I decided I didn't like the looks of her any more than I did her weasel of a father or uncle, or whatever he may be.

"Accompanying my daughter, of course." He looked at the woman with an affectionate smile.

And so I was correct, the unbecoming sight was his daughter. Not caring why they'd chosen to come to the market and keen on changing the view, I said, "I see. Well, do enjoy the rest of your outing. Miss Crawford." I tipped my hat and would've pushed by the pair if his next words hadn't once again paused my flight.

"Rumor has it you now employ a former captain of mine," he hissed like the serpent he was.

I stepped back to level an even stare at him, my jaw clenched so tightly the muscles ached.

"It would only be gentlemanly of me to offer a warning." He extended to his full height.

I arched a brow. "Warning?"

"Yes. No matter the story Gillies may have told you, I had to let him go for thievery."

"Is that so?"

"It is. You see, for a while now I've suspected that someone has been skimming my shipments. The goods have not been reaching the buyers, costing me unspeakable amounts of money and damaging my name. I caught Gillies red-handed, leaving one of my ships with cargo in tow. As one businessman to another, you know I can't have that."

My fingers tenderized the package of mutton I clutched in my hands at his assumption of our similarities. "Thievery amongst your employees cannot be tolerated."

He smiled with smug satisfaction. "I'm glad you agree. Nothing would please me more than to see you send Gillies out into the gutters as he deserves."

"Yes, I'm sure that'd be *very* pleasing to you."

"So, will you?" He waited as though needing an answer.

"Get rid of the captain?" I paused for several seconds, taunting the man.

"That's what I said." The cords of his neck grew rigid.

"I can hardly accuse the man of such a crime without witnessing the thievery firsthand. You can understand that, can't you? Call it gentlemanly honor, if you wish."

The vein in the side of his temple pulsated. "Gillies is not a gentleman. He's the scum congesting our streets. And my word—"

"Means nothing to me. I know of your kind," I said dryly, then willed a charming smile at his daughter. Rattled at the altercation between her father and me, and caught in her open interest in me, she gave me a constrained smile as her cheeks flushed. "Good day, Miss Crawford; Earl." I dodged past them and made my departure, striding assertively over the cobblestones. Triumph surged in my chest at the way Earl's jaw had slackened.

"I won't forget this!" he shouted after me.

I waved a hand in the air. *I'm sure you won't.* The man might attempt to throw his weight around in London, but I for one didn't fear the likes of Earl Crawford. He'd robbed me once of a deal that should've been mine; I'd never allow him a second chance.

I hurried toward the line of waiting hansom cabs and private carriages.

"Mummy, can't I have one?"

The sweetness of a child's voice replaced my annoyance over my encounter with Crawford with a yearning for my daughter. Willow was a sensitive child who sensed when my days were dark and would come seeking to comfort me. Often climbing up on my lap, wordless, she'd cradle her head on my shoulder, and we'd sit molded together, my pain and loneliness subsiding for the moment.

"No, but you may play with them if you like," a woman replied.

I glanced to my right and saw a small girl kneeling beside a box. Furry heads popped over the top of the crate, and I heard the excited whines of puppies.

The girl giggled as a reddish-colored pup licked her hand. "Please, can't I have one?" she pleaded.

"You mustn't push, Callie." The pretty blond woman bent to inspect the critters in the box.

"Look, Mummy, you simply must see." The child didn't look to her left where the blond woman squatted, but lifted her eyes upward.

I followed her gaze, and my heart thudded faster. Standing with her eyes locked on me was Isabella. Her basket of goods lay in a heap on the ground. Fear sheathed her face. Her eyes darted around for an escape route.

I frowned, perplexed and disheartened by her reaction. I swallowed the lump in my throat, all too aware of how I'd left her without an explanation, but the panic I witnessed in her was unsettling.

I strode forward before she could disappear. "Isabella… I've been… It's good to see you."

From the corner of my eye, I saw the other woman stand upright. Isabella's eyes flitted to her and the child. I followed her gaze. The woman stood with a protective arm around her daughter. The child held a wiggling pup in her arms.

"Mummy?" The child looked uncertainly at Isabella.

Mummy? Was the child hers? I studied the girl a moment. Her skin was paler, with a caramel hue, and dark, soft ringlets framed a face much too thin. She had the same eyes as Isabella—a beautiful shade of green with flecks of gold. So it was true: Isabella had found someone.

"What do you have there?" I said to the child.

"A puppy." She beamed while holding it up for my inspection.

"And what a fine little fellow he is." I stroked the head of the pup and willed a cumbersome half-smile at the girl.

She adjusted the weight of the wiggling ball of fur in her arms, and it sent a pink tongue across her nose, securing a string of giggles from her. "He likes me, Mummy."

"Yes, I can see that." Isabella moved with urgency toward her daughter. "Put the puppy back in the box. We must go."

"But Mummy—" the child protested.

"Now!" Isabella said, her body stiff and guarded as she gave her a gentle shove toward the box.

"Do as your mother asks, Callie," the other woman

said, her eyes never leaving me. The tight set of her mouth as she regarded me gave me the impression she knew of me. And what she *believed* she knew wasn't charming.

"Wait!" I said, moving closer. I read the price of the puppies written on the box and turned to the man selling them. I reached inside my coat and retrieved my pocketbook. Withdrawing the exact amount for one puppy, I shoved it at the man. "It appears the pup has taken a liking to the child. We'll take him."

The man grasped the money and tucked it away as the hostility in Isabella's voice spun me around. "No! We can't afford another mouth to feed." She plucked the pup from her daughter's arms and plopped it into mine. Her fingers touched my hand and lingered a hesitant second. Her eyes leaped to mine—searching.

I read her fear. Her panic. Longing. Then she pulled away.

"Come," she said, taking the child by the hand. Tears glistened in the girl's eyes, but she didn't question again. She took one last yearning look at the pup in my arms. I gave the child a grim smile. Guilt rushed through me at my overstepping. I'd harmed the child by giving her the pup for it only to be taken away.

Gripping the pup and my package of mutton, I watched them weave their way toward the carriages.

No! I couldn't let it end like that. I pursued them, spotting them as they scrambled into the seat of a flatbed wagon, pulled by a horse that appeared to be getting on in years. Barely waiting for her passengers to get settled, Isabella cracked the reins, and they were moving away.

I rushed toward a driver who leaned against the side of a hansom cab, waiting on his next customer. "Follow that wagon." I jutted a finger in the direction of the wagon.

The driver went for the door. "No, get us moving." I pulled the door open and climbed inside, pulling the door shut after me.

The carriage lurched forward, and a whine centered my awareness on the squirming bundle in my arms. I gritted my teeth, grumbling under my breath. The pup yelped and looked up at me with an open mouth of shining white spikes and bright eyes. "Great, just what I need," I said to him. Him? Was the critter indeed a male? I held it up in midair to inspect. "That you are."

✑ CHAPTER ✑
Six

Isabella

S ILENCE ENCOMPASSED US LIKE A DENSE FOG AS WE LEFT
London behind. The open fields of the countryside
breathed air into my compressed lungs, and I eased
the horse to a trot. My insides still trembled from the run-
in with Charles.

My stomach had danced and clenched in unison at the
sight of him. The years had powdered his blond locks with
threads of silver, and fine wrinkles had formed around his
lips and the corners of his eyes; the hard line of his jaw
and the sharp ache mirrored in his eyes were unchanging.
I'd thought, with the years apart, the hold he had over me
would've eased, but one look into his eyes had stirred all
the emotions I'd fought years to evict.

When I'd first met him I'd been terrified; he had a
frightening presence, with his serious face and eyes that
dissected your thoughts, invading your darkest secrets.
The week we'd spent together in his townhouse after he
found me in the alley had turned into something neither
he nor I could ever have expected.

The evening I crept down the corridor to thank him

for his kindness and to inform him I was leaving, I'd found him sitting in the parlor. A snifter of brandy gripped in his hand, he'd stared into the mesmerizing flames of the hearth. The demons that pestered him were ever present, and he'd raised the snifter to his lips and emptied the amber liquid.

I'd stood on the threshold, pondering the man whose eyes hooded with the darkness blackening his core. Sensing my presence, he'd looked up with inebriated eyes. Fear gripped me, but to my surprise he'd not become angry. Instead he'd beckoned me to take a seat in the armchair next to him. Too afraid to disobey, I'd sidled over to it.

Hands clasped tightly in my lap, I'd lifted my gaze. His eyes held a profound sadness, something I'd mistaken for hardness. Unsettled under his stare, I dropped my eyes, swallowing back the nerves gathering in my throat.

Maybe it was his loneliness, or another day of submerging his pain in drink, or perhaps the fact he thought he'd never see me again that made him decide to share with me what taxed him. And maybe it was out of fear or building curiosity over what tortured the handsome foreigner that I listened.

He told me of his wife and her love for his brother and the babe conceived from that love. That night, I gave Charles what he required most—friendship and a listening ear. He'd given me sanctuary, and I owed him that much.

During the following days together, he asked of my life and my master, and I believed he found a distraction in doing so. For if his mind was occupied, he didn't have to think of things at home. While we talked, he looked me in the eye and nodded in agreement with my answers to his questions. Until then I'd never been regarded as human by anyone except for my mother and, for the first time, I felt alive. No longer the wallpaper of a mistress's estate, or the sexual release of my master, but a person. Someone of value—not the price paid by a master, but as the whites viewed each other. No station in a household defined me. I was *Isabella*, a guest in Charles Hendricks's home.

"Who was that nice man?" Callie's voice pulled me from the past.

Pippa patted her knee. "A dockworker."

"Why does he talk funny?" Perplexed, she crimped her brow.

Pippa laughed in an attempt to be lighthearted, but I detected the strain in her voice. "He has an accent."

"Where's he from?"

"America," I said, shifting the grip of my damp palms on the reins as I gave Callie a sideways glance.

"Is he your friend?"

"At one time."

"But not anymore?"

"I suppose not."

Her eyes flickered, moving over my face as she silently questioned my response. Puzzlement twisted her mouth, but then, as if satisfied with my answer, she turned to gaze over the pastures, letting the beauty of the country-side and her love for animals carry her young mind to the sheep grazing close to the rock walls skirting both sides of the road. And leaving me to return to my previous thoughts.

Charles had come out of nowhere. Why was he at the market? He was never one for crowds.

As the questions mounted in my head, I felt Pippa's eyes on me. I glanced at her, and she offered me a small, reassuring smile, her eyes promising everything would be all right. But how could they? Charles knew of Callie. Well, not entirely. But he knew she was mine. And that was bad enough. Would he question Mrs. Dier on the matter? What if he put the years together? My heart drummed faster.

"I'm sorry," Pippa said. "I should never have suggested we go in to town."

"It's not your fault."

Callie remained silent but, in a sidelong peek at her, I noticed how her head tilted slightly, as though she were listening. She was far too smart. Raised by Pippa and me, without the companionship of other children, she understood things a child shouldn't at her age.

Later that evening, Callie sat on a chair in front of the fireplace while Pippa combed the tangles from her hair. The flames from the open coal hearth spat and popped, spilling an amber glow over the small room. Callie's honeyed voice sounded out the words in the children's book *Oliver Twist* by Charles Dickens—a gift from Mrs. Dier. When she'd given it to her, I wasn't sure who was more thrilled—Callie or Pippa. Their combined squeal was deafening, and they'd clasped hands and danced around the room.

From the doorway of the bedchamber, I listened to Callie.

"C-a-n. Can." She grinned, pride lifting her small shoulders as she glanced up at Pippa for her approval.

Pippa smiled at her pupil. "That's right."

As Callie continued, I imagined the letters that formed the words she recited. Pride beat in me. My daughter would be educated in all the ways of a real lady. She was learning to read and write. She would have a better life than me. An *X* would not form her name, but instead she'd proudly and confidently scroll her name on all documents with an awareness of what it said.

"All right, it's time for bed, my darling girl," I said.

Callie turned, her eyes gleaming with the reflection of the hearth. Pippa finished tying a single blue ribbon at the bottom of the thick plait holding back Callie's mane of curls. "We will continue your studies tomorrow night." Pippa caressed Callie's cheek with the back of her knuckles.

Callie bobbed her head eagerly, hopped down from the chair with a thud, kissed Pippa's offered cheek, and skipped toward me. "Will you tell me one of your stories?"

"Just one." I held up a finger.

She held up two, mischievousness glinting in her eyes.

"Very well, then it's lids closed for you."

She threw her arms around my waist and declared, her voice muffled, "I love you, Mummy."

I stroked the top of her head and bent to kiss it. "And I you, my love. Now go change into your nightclothes and get under the covers. I'll be right in."

She ambled into the dimly lit room, and I softly closed

the door between the chamber and the main room. Pippa had seated herself on the rocker by the fire and sat observing me.

I took the seat my daughter had vacated. "What has captured your mind?"

"Him."

The mention of Charles sent my nerves racing. "Must we speak of today?"

"I'm baffled."

"How so?"

Her rocker glided smoothly forward and back with calming ease. Never one to get riled up, she proceeded with what was on her mind. "From your desire to avoid speaking of him and the protective way Mrs. Dier has been all these years...I guess I expected him to be a tyrant. But he wasn't. He was, well, kind." A soft groove formed between her perfectly shaped brows. "His eyes held a tenderness for you." Her voice drifted for a second. "And when he realized Callie was yours, confusion shone on his face. Then—"

"He tried to buy her a puppy," I finished for her. "What does a puppy have to do with the grand scheme of things?" I ensured my voice was low so Callie couldn't hear. "He seeded a child with a mulatto woman—an abomination amongst the aristocrats. They'll not look past such a thing. Do not forget, he too owns slaves."

"I understand all this, but maybe we are wrong. Maybe he would provide for her, even if he were never to claim her as his own. I know you want a future for her that doesn't find her scrambling to find food or facing the hardships we've had."

"Of course I don't want that for her. It's just—"

"Just what?" she said. "You know fear is the pit of all undoing. What if you imagine the worst when in fact it could be so much better? He seems civil enough to me, and dashingly handsome to boot." Her eyes sparkled with gaiety.

"I've never known you to be persuaded by dashing good looks." I couldn't help but smile at her.

"Seeing him today changed the image I'd formed in my head of the ghastly man who broke your heart and stole your virtue. And it wasn't his appearance that caused my mind to ponder."

"Neither his looks nor the fact he was cordial changes that he's white and I'm of mixed blood," I said, disheartened. "Besides, Charles will only ever have room for *her* in his heart."

"But she is gone, and you are here." She leaned forward and clasped my hands in hers. Her thumbs tenderly rubbed the tops of my hands, still dark with coal soot.

"Nothing will change that. I gave up on the notion years ago." I heaved a sigh. At first anger had found lodging in my heart at his abandonment, then sadness and, after a few years, resolve.

The door creaked open, Pippa pulled back, and we turned as Callie's head poked out the door. "Mummy, are you coming?"

I rose and patted Pippa's shoulder. "Believe me, I wish things were different. And sometimes," I whispered for her ears only, "I wish not a drop of Negro blood ran through my veins. Then, maybe, we could be together. But then the understanding that he'll always love her, and only her, brings me back to my senses."

She covered my hand on her shoulder with hers and nodded her understanding; sadness darkened her eyes. And I read the hunger she felt for me to be happy and for Callie to secure the father she deserved.

∾ CHAPTER ∾
Seven

Charles

J ULIUS'S EYES HAD NARROWED, AND HIS MOUTH OPENED TO speak when I'd shown up with the mutton and pup in hand, but I'd brushed him off with a grunted "Don't ask" and thrust the meat and the critter into his arms.

The next morning, the pup lay sleeping in front of the hearth while I sat at the table, reading *The Morning Post* and feasting on crumpets and coffee. A pitiful whine from the pup drew my eyes to where he lay, his legs twitching. Dreams chased him, as they often did me. I suspected his were less troublesome.

Dreams of Olivia had not come to me last night. Instead, I'd tossed and turned, knotting the bed linens as visions of Isabella and the child seized my subconscious.

"Julius!" I called, and lifted my cup of coffee to my mouth. I'd grown accustomed to the man lurking, waiting in some darkened corner of the house for my next command. His footsteps often went undetected, and when he uttered "Sir?" I jerked in my seat and coffee splashed on my upper lip and dripped down my chin. I choked back the curse on the tip of my tongue and lifted my napkin to dab my face. *Blasted man needs to wear a bell!*

"See to it that my horse is saddled and ready to go. I'm going to be taking a ride in the country today."

He stood with his head bowed, never lifting his gray eyes to meet mine. "W-wouldn't you find a carriage more suitable for your comfort? It's a mite c-chilly out there."

"If I thought a carriage would be more suitable, I would have requested one."

"Yes, sir. Your steed w-will be ready," he said, appearing unmoved by my sour disposition.

I felt a pang of guilt. I recalled a time when he'd greeted me with a grand smile and excited chatter at my arrival—a time when we'd engaged as though we were friends. When I'd been younger, with a zest for life and what awaited me around the next adventure. But that was before, and this was now. Years had curved such interactions, and I ran my staff and households as it should be—as servants and the master.

Unnerved by the emptiness lodging in me like a bloated storm cloud, I grunted a reply, threw my napkin on the table, and pushed to my feet. I slipped past him and strode toward the stairs to change.

An hour later, I left the dreariness of the city behind and rode down the road toward the cottage the driver had followed Isabella and her companions to the previous day.

I reined the horse to a halt at the edge of the tree line. The simple homestead sat alone in the valley below, a speck in the vast farmland surrounding it, like a lone ship in the vast sea. I spied a neighboring farm in the distance. The farmer's sheep roamed the hills, bleating and feeding on the once-lush green carpet that had faded with the changing of seasons. *For all creatures, humans, and living things, there is a time and a season,* I thought, *and time goes on, and seasons change despite one's readiness. And soon the snow will come, and I set sail for America in two days.*

Below, I spotted the blond woman from the market; she stumbled toward the cottage under the weight of a thick tree limb that rested across her shoulders with a pail suspended on each end. A hired carriage sat in front of the home. Jealousy rose in me. Was it the man Isabella was to marry? The emotion had no sooner surged before I pushed it away. I had no right to such sentiments.

I turned my head at the creaking of approaching wagon wheels on the gravel road behind me. Nudging my heels into my mount, I urged him to the side of the road as an elderly man driving a flatbed wagon drew near. An idea hit me, and I moved my horse back into the path of the oncoming cart.

"Good day, sir," I said with a tip of my hat as he reined his team of oxen to a stop.

"What in the blazes are you doing blocking the road?" His upper lip curled in, cupping his gums where teeth had once been.

"I need your help."

"And you expect you're going to gain my help by holding up my day?" he grumbled, his lips smacking with displeasure.

"I suppose not. But I assure you, this won't take but a moment of your time."

"Then get on with it. I got milk to deliver." He jerked his head at the wagon bed of milk drums.

I gestured to the cottage. "You know the folks that live there?"

He looked past me to the cottage and then back, his brow wrinkled, his posture stiffening. "Certainly; they're my neighbors. What do you want with them?"

"I'm looking to hire a seamstress." I swatted the fly that settled on the mane of the bay with my riding stick.

His face relaxed, yet remained uninviting, the channels that marked his flesh as deep as if carved with a blade. Years of hard work under the unrelenting sun had left their mark. "I suppose you come to the right place. That filly makes some of the finest clothing around. Got the uppitiest of folks coming right to her front door."

"They come all the way out here?" *Well, I'll be! She's done well for herself.* This information pleased me. "She must be talented," I said. "London is filled with tailors."

"And to think she was once a slave." He shook his head in admiration. "That one can take care of herself. And since Miss Pippa moved in a few years back and helps her out around the place and with the girl, I expect things might be a tad bit easier on the poor girl."

"This Pippa, who is she?"

"I ain't sure." He removed his hat and scratched his head. "The gents at the country tavern say she's none other than the eldest daughter of his lordship Samuel Buxton."

I couldn't place the name, but it sounded familiar. "The child. She has no father?"

The man's openness of moments ago evaporated and he eyed me with distrust, sitting up straighter on the seat. "Why you be asking? If you're claiming to be here with the interest of hiring the seamstress, what's it to you?"

I said in all seriousness, regardless of the lie I breathed, "I was raised without a pa. No siblings. My ma worked her fingers to the bone to make sure I didn't go hungry."

"I see." He wasn't soaking up the story I wove to tug at his heart.

I rushed on to feed him a fabricated story of my life in hopes of setting him at ease. "Spent my whole life working the streets, trying to earn a living after my ma died. Even had a job as a rat catcher in New York for a short spell when I was a young lad. Then life smiled at me one day shortly after my twentieth year, and I met my wife. By then I'd become a captain and she was a passenger on my ship, recently widowed and lonely. Often at night she'd come on deck and stroll, lost in thought. I watched her for several nights until one night she caught me, her head tilted, and she studied me. I stared back, awestruck at her beauty, and then instead of turning away, she moved toward me." He'd leaned forward. I'd captured him. I continued. "Each night after she'd come on deck and seek me out, and the rest, after that, you can guess."

"Though life seems to have worked out for you," his gaze roved over my attire and mount, "I guess you might know what it's like to go without like the rest of us. All stories don't get a happy ending like yours, but I don't be faulting you for your strike of good luck."

Luck! I smirked to myself. Luck had never been on my side. If it had, life would have been very different. Bitterness rolled over my tongue, sour and ripe.

"I got milk to deliver," he said.

"Yes. My apologies. Good day, sir." I tipped my hat and moved to the side of the road.

He waved a hand, grunted something inaudible, and whipped the reins, and the oxen lumbered down the road.

I turned my gaze back to the cottage, pausing a second to reflect on my decision to show up in Isabella's life after so much time had passed. The questions that had kept me awake long into the night coursed through my head. Was I doing what was right? Or was I fulfilling a selfish need within myself?

I nudged my horse forward to make the descent to the cottage, planning to avoid the lane and the risk of the occupants spotting my approach and taking to the hills to hide.

Chickens scurried around the front yard and, to the left of the house, a lone cow stood in the small pasture. The happy chattering of a child came from somewhere outside. I dismounted and tied my horse to the fence post next to the cow, who peered at me with her all-seeing, dark-lashed eyes. I stroked her head before turning toward the sound of the child. My heart thumped in my ears as I strode up to the iron gate to the right of the home. The child from the market sat on the stone path, playing with a shabby-looking doll; a pretty blue dress, lovingly made, I suspected, clothed the toy, but the body and face were dirty from play.

The child, dressed in a simple graying smock and woolen mittens, was unaware of my presence. As though I were a kidnapper ready to prey on the girl, I peered around for eyewitnesses. Finding no one, I turned my attention back to the child. For a moment I observed her, lost in the innocence of her play, and reflected on a time when my brother and I were young boys and life wasn't as complicated. How your greatest wish is to get older, unaware of the burdens that come with age! Time is the most precious thing one can own, and yet I'd wished it all away.

"If you want to hear a story, you must get ready for bed," the child said to the doll. Her voice changed to a whine. "But I don't want to."

I'd seen such play with my own daughter, and I found myself smiling at the way children mimicked their parents in play.

As if suddenly sensing my presence, she looked up at me with big green eyes the shade of wild ferns. She frowned and craned her neck while studying me with interest. Then a smile escaped her and a twinkle of mischievousness animated her eyes. "Hello," she said.

"Hello." My voice came out gruff and I willed a smile, not wanting to intimidate the girl. Henrietta had informed me, on more than one occasion, that I had a way of frightening children. I'd observed the way her daughter, Mary Grace, would cling to Willow or her mama's skirt at my appearance. The truth was, I wasn't good with children. They'd always made me nervous. But Willow had found a way to wiggle under the shield I'd erected to ward off vulnerability and hurt and placed her handprint on my heart.

"I'm looking to speak to your mama," I said, trying my very best to make my voice soft; instead it came out like a rusty hinge in bad need of oiling.

The child appeared unaffected by my gruffness and rose. "Did you bring the puppy?" Her eyes darted past me as if she expected to find him trailing behind me.

Something in the child's determination to possess the dog reminded me of Willow, and an awkward low chortle escaped me. "No."

"Mummy says I can't have the puppy." Her shoulders slumped.

"Your mother knows best."

"What did you call him?"

"Dog."

Her brow dropped. "You can't call him Dog."

"What do you suppose I should call him?"

She thought a moment, then said, "Red. No, wait! Beau."

"Beau?"

"Because he is beautiful. Miss Pippa says that in Paris, 'beau' means handsome."

I laughed. "Very well. I shall call him Beau."

She smiled, and then another concern seemed to skip into her mind and the smile slipped. "Who will play with him?"

And so this was the problem with children and their

endless supply of questions. "My daughter," I said with patience foreign to me.

"What's her name?"

"Willow."

"Hmm," she said. Then, as if satisfied with her investigation into the pup's future, she turned and raced down the stone path. "Mummy, that dock man is here."

CHAPTER
Eight

Isabella

THE NEEDLE PIERCED MY FINGER WHEN I HEARD CALLIE'S call. But the pain didn't register. I sat frozen, the frock I'd been mending clutched in my hands. *Charles. Here? No, it can't be.* How had he found us? But as the questions rolled through my mind, I already knew the answer. He'd followed us, I was sure of it.

The side door to the room burst open and Callie trudged in, her eyes bright with the excitement of a guest. "Mummy, he's here!" she said. "The man from the market."

A shadow overtook her. I jumped to my feet, the gown I'd clutched dropping in a pile at my feet. "Hello, Isabella?" Charles removed his hat and stood in the doorway, a kind smile curving his lips.

And there he stood, in my home, with our daughter but a finger's reach away. Panic seized my chest. *Close. Too close.* My heart pounded, almost painfully so. "Charles." I swallowed hard. "W-what are you doing here?" My voice quavered.

Callie looked from me to him. She had always been in tune to my emotions and, when she looked at me, worry reflected in her eyes. "He didn't bring the puppy," Callie said as though that would make him welcome.

"And risk your mother throwing him back at me and running off? No. I left the pup at my home," he said.

"Mummy says you're from America and that is why you talk funny. And that you're a dockworker."

Charles's eyes turned to me. "Did she, now? I suppose I am a dockworker of sorts."

Suddenly, air pumped through my lungs. I gasped and said with urgency, "Callie, go find Pippa."

"But Mummy—"

"Do it now!" My words came out harsher than intended. Callie stiffened, and I winced. I went to her and capped her shoulder with a hand. "Please, luv—"

The door separating the main room from the back room swung open and Pippa and Mrs. Dier barged in, their faces shocked at the sight of Charles.

"Why, Mrs. Dier, fancy meeting you here!" Charles said dryly.

"Mr. Hendricks, I-I—"

"Pippa, Mrs. Dier, please take Callie. I will deal with this." I gave Callie a nudge toward them, and I was grateful when she went without a fuss.

"Are you sure?" Pippa asked, looking from Charles to me, as Mrs. Dier led Callie from the room.

I nodded. With concern shining in her blue eyes and a firm press of her lips, Pippa gave Charles a warning look before closing the door.

"I-Isa…" Charles said.

I turned, avoiding his gaze. "I'll fetch my shawl, and

then we will take a walk, and you will tell me why you followed us." I spun on my heel, opened the door, and went to grab my shawl on the peg by the door in the main room.

The women and Callie sat at the table, unmoving, holding their breath as I entered the room and exited as swiftly as I'd come.

Charles stood outside the back room in the garden, waiting. Without a word, I strode to the wrought iron gate and opened it, stepped out, and waited for him to follow. We walked in silence, moving toward the open fields until we reached the rock wall overgrown with foliage that would shield us from view from the cottage. Many days I'd come to this exact spot to think, and often worry, away from the keen eyes of Pippa. I halted, pulled the shawl tightly around me, and turned to him. His footfalls ceased, and for a moment only the chirping of birds, an occasional bleat from the sheep, and the burbling of the stream behind him broke the silence.

"Why have you come?" I said, willing myself to look him in the eyes—only to be taken aback by the tenderness I read in them.

"I know it's impolite to show up uninvited. Please forgive me, but I've been searching for you. I've asked Mrs. Dier, but as I'm sure you are already aware, her loyalty is unbreakable."

"She has informed me of your attempts at locating me," I said. "I often wondered why. I am no longer your apprentice, therefore you are no longer tied to me in any way." *Except for the daughter we share.* "What is it you want?"

"I want to make things right," he said, looking down

at his fingers pressing the brim of his hat. "I behaved poorly...how I left you—it wasn't right. I've had years to think of what I would say if I were to find you. Emotions of the heart aren't easy for me and well, I..." His struggle to speak what was on his mind overwhelmed him and he looked past me to the rolling landscape. He opened his mouth to continue, then pressed his lips together. His jaw tightened in that oh-so-familiar way. When he spoke next, the tenderness of his words pulled the threads I'd sewn over my heart. "I—I was scared. The emotions you stirred in me were beyond frightening." His eyes captured my face. "Fate brought us together in a time when I needed a friend; a confidant. Why? I don't know. But when I reflect on our times together, I think of them fondly. That night... the night we moved past friendship..." Again his thoughts drifted.

The night I conceived your daughter.

"I panicked," he continued. "I can't allow myself to love you. If I did it would only bring about pain and heartbreak for us both. I don't need to tell you that our parentage is one reason, but it goes deeper than that. I could never—"

"Love me like you did her," I finished for him. *Still do,* I wanted to add.

He inclined his head and heaved a sigh. "It's not fair to you. I know how it feels to love someone whose heart belongs to another. I care enough for you to know I don't wish that for you."

He didn't know how I would've settled for a piece of his heart. The safety I felt when I was around him far outweighed the desire to own all of his heart. "But you have no control over that. You can't stop someone from falling in love. If I could, I would've stopped myself from falling for you. What happened between us should never have happened. You're a master of slaves, and I was once a slave. A future for us would be doomed from the start. My life is here in England and yours is in America, where slavery is alive and thriving." The finality in my words left a silence between us. We stood lost in our own thoughts.

"Mrs. Dier tells me you're to be married," he said.

"Married?" The word came out before I could shove it back in. Mrs. Dier had told me she'd led him to believe I was to marry, in hopes of making him give up his mission to find me.

"It isn't true?'

"No. Well, yes." I hesitated. "No. I am not to wed. Mrs. Dier forged that story to stop your search."

Amusement gleamed in his eyes. "Old crow!" he said almost affectionately. "Witty one, that one."

I laughed. "That she is."

He grew serious. "If you are not to marry then, may I ask, who's the father of the child?"

I stiffened. His brow dipped low. "What is it? Someone didn't...did someone harm you?" he said sharply, squaring his shoulders.

"No," I replied, just above a whisper. I fought within myself to tell him the truth. He'd lost so much already; was it right to keep his daughter from him? But what if he became angry at my withholding of the fact? Or became enraged that he'd fathered a child with me at all.

The tall grass around us rustled, and I felt his hands cup my shoulders. "Isabella." His voice was soft and summoning, his touch gentle as he lifted my chin. "What is it?"

I looked deep into his eyes, searching; peeling back the many layers to the perplexed man who stood before me. He cared for me. And I believed he loved me. Not in the way a person does a soulmate, but as one cares for a dear friend. The way I did for Pippa. Life had bound us together, not only through friendship but our daughter, and in this understanding I found the courage to tell him the truth. "She is yours."

I felt his body grow rigid and I tensed. "Mine?" he said. His hands dropped, and he took a staggering step backward. "But how?" Then his eyes grew large. "Are you sure? I mean…" He ran a hand over his face and pulled it down. He paced a circle, not waiting for my answer, and as the possibility sank in, he paused and turned back. "Sweet Jesus…"

I folded my arms across my chest to quell the trembling rocking my body. Taking a deep breath, I said, "I did not tell you because—well, you left. And I thought you were ashamed of that night we spent together—bedding the help and all."

His eyes flew to me. "You weren't that to me," he said, as though insulted that I'd say such a thing. "I didn't see it like that." His voice was gentler and pained.

"Let's not get caught up on what we can't change. I loved you, and I suppose I always will. I bore a daughter out of that love and, for that, I am not ashamed. Callie's my gift from you. In her, I have a part of you, and I've accepted that's all I'll ever have. I ask of you, please don't take her from me. She's all I have." Tears came to me then. Pools of them. Years of tears. Of pain. And loneliness. I missed him and having him so close, I wanted to kiss him and feel the strength and safety within his embrace. Through my tears, I said, "I do not expect you to claim her as your heir." Then I wept, hiding the shame of my weakness behind my hands, my body convulsing as the sobs overtook me.

"Isabella," he said with a groan, and then his arms embraced me. His lips whispered his tortured words. "I wish I could offer you more...I wish I could let her go, but I can't. God help me, but I can't!"

I wept harder. *I know...* And in one shallow breath I hated the woman who owned his soul, and in the next, I grieved to know the greatness of a woman who'd won the man I had at one time so desperately wanted to love me.

And in his honesty my respect for the father of my daughter and a man that would always have my heart grew. I allowed myself the comfort of his embrace, and for a moment we were the runaway slave and the broken man who sat in front of the fireplace all those years ago, lost in the addiction of the togetherness we felt in each other's presence. Though we would never again be lovers, I realized I wanted more than anything to continue the friendship we had started before we allowed weakness to get in the way. The thought of another year or a lifetime without him constricted my chest.

I stepped back and smiled up at him. He smiled in

the restricting way Charles Hendricks was capable of before lifting a thumb and wiping the tears from the corners of my eyes. I laughed tightly and patted my cheeks.

"Can we agree to be friends?" I asked.

"Back to where we started?" he said. "Yes, I'd like that very much." He offered his arm and the hooded gaze I had become accustomed to returned. "Let's take a walk while I adjust to this news."

I cupped my hand in the crook of his elbow, he slid his hand over mine, and the warmth and the strength from his hand calmed the disquiet within me. For hours Charles and I walked the fields, renewing a friendship that had withstood time and distance.

When Charles had purchased me, the law had bound us together. From afar I had admired a man who owned me as one would property. Then, as fate would have it, we built a relationship based on mutual trust and respect only to be torn apart by his fear to love again. But, in the end, I'd found a friendship that I hoped would expand through the years to come. And regardless of the years that passed, Charles *was* still the man I believed him to be. He had rescued me and I liked to think I'd rescued him…

ᏹ CHAPTER ᏹ
Nine

Charles

THE SUN WAS SETTLING ON THE HORIZON BY THE TIME I returned to London. My head felt muddled with the daunting revelations of the afternoon and, as habit would have it, I found myself pulling my mount to a halt at the docks. Whether on my ships moored in some harbor or at sail, in the calm of the water I found the refuge I craved. At sea, the anchor wedged in my heart released, and I was somewhat whole, the man I was before Olivia; the man with hope for the future, not tormented and adhering to the past and the ghost of my wife. Not grieved by a lifetime of choices made out of fear of losing what was never meant to be mine from the start.

But it wasn't the internal self-punishment I inflicted on myself over my failure to protect my wife or the frayed relationship between my brother and me that harassed me that evening as I strolled the dock. Instead, the darker-skinned child playing with the doll on the stone pathway captured my thoughts.

I paused and rested my hands on the rail stretching along the dock. The waves of the harbor lapped against the wharf, mimicking the pumping inside my chest. *Blast it!* My hands curled into fists on the rail. What was I to do now? I couldn't just leave for home without somehow providing for the girl. Nor could I claim a child with Negro blood as my own. Olivia had died with the secret of her involvement with the Underground Railroad, and I'd done everything within my power to cover it up. I'd broken the law and taken another man's property and gotten them far away from Charleston. If I were branded a Negro lover too, it would be the end of all I'd worked for—my ships would be seized, and life without the sea at my back was no life at all. Prison or a hate mob's noose would surely be my fate.

And then what would become of Willow? At the thoughts of harm coming to my daughter, my heart thumped faster, and my teeth gnawed at the corner of my mouth. *Never! I'd give my life before I'd*—A low cry vibrated in my chest. She was the reason I still drew breath each day.

My parents were gone, and to my knowledge, Ben and Willow were the last of our family. The ultimatum I had placed on him and Olivia had been the final divide between my brother and me. I had not seen him since the day he showed up after I sent the letter telling him to come to Livingston immediately.

That day, from the doorway of my study, I'd watched him reel back at the sight of Willow playing with Mary Grace on the floor in the parlor. I hadn't expected him to arrive so swiftly and rose from my seat, instinct warning me to grab Willow and protect what was mine, but my feet remained riveted to the floor. The look of longing and loss that had swept over Ben's face filled me with remorse and self-loathing. But the notion of losing the last piece of Olivia had been my broken compass. Though Ben could've taken Willow then and time would have eased me from her memories as it had her mother, he'd done what was right for her. Could I say the same? He'd not wanted to take the one thing she had left, the only father she'd ever known. And I'd detested him for his selflessness. His continued heroism was like a knife in my side. I couldn't bear the sight of him. The hollowness reflected in his eyes of his sacrifice was mirrored by all the wrongs I'd done to the brother that had once been my closest friend. He was a man more remarkable than all that would come after him, and I loved him. The ache of missing him was a feeling I'd become skilled at pushing away.

I hadn't been ready to face the responsibility of raising Willow alone, but I wasn't strong enough to give her to the man I'd never measure up to. I loved Willow more than anything I had in this world, and for so long it had just been her and me—until now.

But what of the child, Callie? What was her future?

Never would I have imagined my search for Isabella would lead to this discovery. How I'd longed to see her, to rest in the ease of her company. To look into her eyes and become lost in the honesty that dwelt within her. I'd confided in her about Willow's conception and the murder of my wife. She knew the ugly truth about me and still she had loved and befriended me. To be loved by someone was a feeling I'd long forgotten. Emotions clogged in my throat.

A scuffle inside a building behind me followed by the cries of a woman carried above the sound of the waves licking against the moored ships and wharf.

"Please, no! I am a freed woman. You can't do this. Help!" She let out a scream before her cries were muffled. I stood riveted by the wail. Then I moved closer, dodging into the shadows of the building.

"Keep her quiet, you damn fool," a man said in a low hiss. "Crawford will have our heads if we mess this up. With my missus due any day, I can't afford to lose this money."

"Aye. But maybe Gillies is right. Maybe we shouldn't be helping Crawford take folks from the streets."

"Gillies!" The man's voice grew louder before he caught himself and returned to hushed tones. "If you turn coward like him, I'll kill you myself." At the mention of Crawford and Gillies I inched closer to hear.

"No need to get all testy. I'm only saying, what if it was your missus and child we ripped from the streets this night?"

"Joe, I swear if you start growing a conscience—"

I knocked over a spade and the metal rattled on the wharf. *Dammit all to hell!* I looked for a hiding spot to squeeze into.

"Go check it out," one of the men said.

I darted down the wharf and leaped in between rows of crates stacked for shipping as door hinges creaked behind me. Still a head's height above the crates, I crouched as low as I could go, my body protesting the cramped quarters. I held my breath as feet tromped down the wharf in my direction. In the gap between crates, I watched the man as he came to a halt and stood scanning the dock.

After what seemed like hours he mumbled something inaudible and jogged back the way he'd come. After he was gone, I released the breath straining my lungs and slipped from between the crates. I headed toward my office at the end of the wharf. Inside, I lit a lantern and took a seat behind my desk.

So Gillies was right. Crawford was taking the poor from the streets and illegally selling them.

A chill galloped through me as visions of Callie at the market, stroking the puppies in the box, and her at play outside of the cottage were marred with the thoughts of Crawford capturing her and selling her to a master. The strike of the whip on her delicate flesh. Her soul empty and the glimmer of childlike innocence replaced with the emptiness of a slave. My fingernails bit into the palms of my hands. Shame of who I was and the lives I molded in my hands with each purchase of humans rested heavy with me.

For the first time since I had held Olivia's body that day, I wept. Not for the loss of my wife, but for the lives that had been affected by my hand. And for what I knew in my heart I had to do.

Exhausted and void of emotions, sleep eventually came to me. I awoke hours later. Julius would be beside himself with worry that I hadn't returned. Retrieving my hat, I turned down the lantern and exited the office.

"It's as I told you," a man said outside. I jumped, taken by surprise. Recognizing Gillies's voice, I searched the darkness until my eyes settled on the red glow of a cigar. He stood with his knee lifted and his foot resting against a crate. Beside him stood my horse with his head dipped into a bucket of grain.

"What are you referring to?" I said as he stepped forward.

"What went down at Crawford's warehouse last evening."

"Were you following me?" I said.

"Nay. I'm most at home on these docks. I come here to think and watch the comings and goings at night. Saw you bolting down the docks, then what came after, and recognized Crawford's puppets."

"I'm guessing you saw them exit with a woman?"

"Aye. A Negro woman and a child. Took them aboard *Caliber* and belowdecks shortly after you ducked in here. I brought his fella down here, out of sight. Don't want them to blame you for what I intend to do."

"And what is that?"

"Take what doesn't belong to him."

"Do not forget you work for me. You getting caught trespassing on Crawford's ships would reflect on me."

"Aye, sir. But I don't plan on getting caught."

The Ainsworths' banquet proved to be a trying event. Surrounded by gentleman acquaintances who engaged in political and business discussions that normally held my attention, this evening was lost on me. Their voices jumbled together as I pondered on the conversation I'd had with Gillies earlier that day

"Comes a time in life when you can't just exist. You got to start living. Got to do something that matters," he'd said.

His words plagued me, coming atop Isabella's revelation that had sent the earth spinning. Maybe there was truth in Gillies's words. I had to find a purpose in life. To see a reason to exist beyond my love for Willow. To feel the exhilaration of life pound in my chest again and quell the desire to flee from the problems life had been relentless in sending my way.

"Mr. Hendricks, we meet again." Crawford's voice pulled me from my musing.

"So we do," I said.

"How's business?" another man asked Crawford.

"As good as can be expected with these foreigners creeping in on our territory," he said to the gentleman, never glancing at me. I knew to whom his remark was intended.

"Yet the British Empire imposes itself on China," I scoffed. "Importing chests of opium by the boatload into the country. Foreign traders who *illegally* flood the China markets with opium. Is the British Empire not responsible for the war between your countries? But you, Mr. Crawford, are no stranger to illegal trade, are you not?"

Crawford's eyes slit. "What are you implying?"

"That you illegally take people from the streets and sell them into slavery and servitude when both are a crime in Britain. I believe just last evening I saw one of your ships moored in the harbor under the guise of a Portuguese flag. My source says that the ship is headed to Brazil in the morning."

Gasps came from the men in our circle and Crawford become rigid, his eyes firing a warning. "I know not what you speak of."

"Oh, but we both know you do," I said.

"If it were true, what would it matter to you, American?"

"It doesn't. I'm merely making a point. You involve yourself in illegal trade in this country and others, so don't judge me."

"Are you seeking to make an enemy of me?"

"I do not wish to make an enemy of you, nor do I wish to be your friend, but I do find it irritating when my competitors don't apply ethics to their trading. It makes it harder for the rest of us"—I gestured toward the other gentlemen—"to do business."

"Mr. Hendricks has a point," one said.

Crawford glowered at him and then whipped his head back to me. "Don't impose your opinions where they aren't needed. It'd do you well to stay out of affairs that don't concern you."

"And it would do you well to conduct your business accordingly, or I'll see to it that you are ousted for the fraudulent businessman you are," I said without skipping a beat.

"Consider yourself warned," he said.

"Noted." I waved a hand and offered a half bow.

He marched off and found a corner on the far side of the ballroom. I studied Crawford while he paced, his lips moving as he engaged in a dialog with himself.

I should ruin that cheating bastard once and for all!

"You have guts, to go up against a man like Crawford," said Daniel Barlow as the other men engaged in conversations of their own. I looked at him. He was a man who'd found pleasure in art and, to my recollection, had never invested in the trading of goods. The inner contentment I saw in his eyes gave me respite, and I considered what it might be like to find fulfillment within yourself. I envied the man.

"His kind makes my insides bleed," I said, looking at Crawford to find his focus had turned to a pretty Negro servant girl. He'd most likely steal the girl right out from under the noses of her employers. I envisioned him tallying the profit he could make from her. Anxiety crested in me, and I lifted a finger to casually wipe the sweat pearling on my upper lip.

"Come," Barlow said. "Gentlemen, if you'll excuse us, I want to speak to Mr. Hendricks about purchasing a few of my paintings." They waved their acknowledgment, and I followed him down an empty corridor. He turned to me when we were out of the earshot of guests. "Is what you say true? Does Crawford pillage the poor?"

I nodded. "Saw his men last night on the docks."

"And why does it matter to you?" His forwardness was unwavering. "Is it your intent to simply humiliate the man?"

I quite liked a man that stood firm in himself and without reservation challenged me. "Partially," I said. "I will ask you the same: Why do my dealings with Crawford concern you?"

"I'm curious why a man who is a slave owner would give a moment's hesitation to another man's dabbling in the trade. I'd expect some of his customers are Americans."

"I do not do trade with men like Earl Crawford. Nor do I wish to victimize the vulnerable or underprivileged."

"Yet you own slaves."

His words burned like those I'd heard from no abolitionist person I'd encountered before, and I ducked my head to conceal how his words found residence in me. My wife died defending the Negros while I visited auctions to purchase them. Was I any better a man than Crawford? The realization of our similarities unnerved me. *"Comes a time when one must change,"* Gillies chimed in my head.

"You are right," I said, lifting my head. "And you haven't?"

"Never. To own another man is a sin and a crime against mankind. How could I be a true artist that sees the beauty in the world if my soul is poisoned with hate?"

"Hate?"

"Only hate and the thirst for power could drive a man to seek ownership of another."

Hate? Was that not the look I'd read in Crawford's eyes when he spat out the word "Negro"? Why now did Barlow's question trouble me so? Never before had opinions from people of his nature halted my thoughts or actions. To succeed and profit had been my aspiration. Until the last day, such philosophies had never found a foothold in me. I had never stopped and considered if I too had become a victimizer of the people I had viewed as profit. Gutted, I stood before him without an answer.

The collar of my shirt felt strangling and I tugged at it. "If you will excuse me, I think I'll take my leave. I head home in the morning."

"Safe journey." His hand gripped my shoulder, and I looked him in the eye. "We all make choices in life. It's never too late to choose a new direction," he said, as though he were reading the battle within me.

I held out a hand, and he grasped it with sincerity. "Until we meet again," I said.

He nodded, and I made my departure.

In the study at my townhouse an hour later, I sat at my desk scripting a letter. After signing my name, I folded the parchment, slid it into an envelope, and sealed it with a knob of wax into which I pressed my family crest.

"Julius!" I called, pushing back from my desk.

He darkened the threshold moments later. "Yes, Mr. Hendricks."

"Are my trunks ready?"

"Yes, sir. And I've summoned the driver. He is w-waiting for you."

"Much obliged."

"Surely you can w-wait until the morn to set sail."

"No. We leave tonight. Captain Gillies has prepared the vessel and gathered the crew."

"W-when can we ex-p-pect your return?"

"In the spring," I said. "Tomorrow, I need this letter delivered to a cottage in the country. I've written down directions on how to get there."

"I'll have the driver deliver it tomorrow."

"No, this is a matter I need you to personally attend to."

"Certainly, sir. It w-will be done as requested."

I caught his eye. "You've been a loyal employee of this household, and I wish to increase your wage to one more fitting."

He inclined his head. "Thank you kindly, sir."

"Very well. See to it my trunks are loaded."

After he was gone, I stood to stare at the empty doorway, lost in contemplation of what I was about to do until a whine at my feet demanded my attention. The pup rubbed his long velvet ears against my leg as if to rid himself of an itch before standing on his hind legs and stretching up to paw at my knees. I bent and pulled him into my arms, stroking the back of his head. "Let's see how you fare in a life at sea." He let out a yelp and cocked his head as if trying to figure out what I had said. I grinned.

Later I stepped outside and tipped my head to peer at the sky. A snowflake melted on the tip of my nose. The shivering pup in my arms lapped up the flakes falling around us. I opened my tweed frock coat and tucked the critter inside before making my descent down the back steps and through the gate to the livery yard where the carriage waited.

❦

I stood on the deck of the *Olivia II* as London faded away into the black of the night. I hoped Isabella would understand my reasoning for setting sail early and that I wasn't running from my duty as a father, that this time my sudden departure had meaning and purpose.

"Masa," a man said.

I turned to find a Negro sailor waiting for my command.

"Masa, what we gonna do wid dem?" He motioned to the people huddled on the deck by the main mast. The Negro woman and child Gillies had said were the ones I'd heard the other night, and the Irish woman and her three children, had been plucked from slums by the dock. Gillies had found them chained in the hold of Crawford's ship.

I moved closer to the women and children, and the colored woman put a protective hand on the sleeping toddler cradled in her lap while the other mother eyed me with ardor in her eyes. I had yet to figure out what I intended to do with the lot, but when I'd agreed to help Gillies rescue them from a fate I could only assume would be worse I had acted without giving heed to what I would do after I secured Crawford's merchandise.

"It won't be an easy journey below deck, but it will have to do. You will be well fed and cared for. Neither my men nor I will harm you. When we reach America, I will see to it that harm does not befall you. You will not be sold and forced into any deed out of your control." As I made this promise, I grasped how much I wanted to keep that promise. How...I didn't yet know but, in honor of what Olivia had died trying to do and to protect children like the one I shared with Isabella, I'd do my part in aiding folks without the means to defend themselves.

The Negro woman spoke. "Ain't America the heart of slavery?"

"It is."

"How you expect the place to be any better?"

"I can't promise it will be. But I can assure you, with me, you have a chance at a future brighter than the one Crawford intended for you."

The woman fell silent, and I gestured for the sailor to get them to their feet. The colored child awoke and protested with a whine at the disturbance. The mother patted the child's head, placing her lips to her forehead. "We be all right now," she said, holding my gaze for a moment before turning and following the sailor down the narrow steps into the darkness below.

I ran a trembling hand over my face. *I hope you know what you are doing.* I knew there was no going back from what Gillies and I had set in motion, but by the time Crawford recuperated from a night of drink we would be far out at sea. He may suspect I'd duped him, but there was no proof. I'd set sail a few hours earlier than schedule, was all.

At the side of the ship, I rested my hands on the rail and gazed into the darkness that had swallowed London. Isabella's face and kind eyes came to me. "I promise...I'll be back." The evening breeze captured my whisper, but as I breathed the words I'd never been surer of anything in my life. London held purpose. I would not abandon Isabella and Callie because, like Willow, I owed them.

CHAPTER
Ten

Isabella

LIGHT SNOW HAD FALLEN OVERNIGHT AND STRETCHED across the fields, revealing winter's promise. It was early evening, and I stood washing the supper dishes in a basin on the table while Pippa added the last of our coal to the hearth. A knock sounded on the door. I glanced at Pippa, whose face mirrored my confusion at who could be visiting at that time of night. I shrugged, dried my hands on my apron, and went to the door.

Opening the door, I gasped, "Julius? W-what are you doing here?"

Charles's butler stood with his hat resting in the crook of his arm, a hint of a frown knitting his brow before he quickly gathered his composure. A grimace touched his mouth as he adjusted his weight from one foot to the other, and I recalled the bouts of pain he suffered during the cold season. "It's...b-been a long time," he said.

I looked past him, brushing back stray hairs from my face. "Is Charles with you?"

He cleared his throat. "H-he is gone."

Gone? But... An ache I'd put in the past resurfaced. I had hoped... What had I expected? That Charles would stand by his promises—yes, that is what I had believed. Heat enveloped my face, and I dropped my head to hide my humiliation once again from Julius. *Flee! It's what you do best!* My throat thickened.

"H-he asked me to give you this." He held out an envelope. "I meant to bring it sooner in the day, but matters needed to be attended to and I found myself trying to b-beat the dark to get it to you. Mr. Hendricks asked me to deliver it personally. I'm sorry for the delay."

I took the letter from his outstretched hand and lifted my head. "Do come in out of the cold." Stepping aside, I gestured to one of the rockers in front of the hearth.

"That's awful nice of you, miss, but I must get back. My old bones don't care for this w-weather no more than they do the carriage ride."

"Then I wish you well."

He replaced his hat and stepped back. "Good evening." He turned and strode toward the carriage, opened the door, and climbed inside.

Later I sat in front of the hearth, wrapped in a quilt to ward off the chill. Callie's soft snores drifted from the open door of the bedroom and Pippa sat across from me in a rocker, reading. Or pretending to read; I'd caught her eyeing me around the book as I allowed the flames of the fire to steal my thoughts. In my hands I gripped the thick envelope Julius had delivered earlier in the day, too afraid to find out what was within. Was this Charles's final goodbye? Regret had loomed over me since Julius had informed me Charles had headed back to America. I should never have told him.

"How long will you torture yourself?" Pippa closed her book and laid it in her lap. "Open the letter and put you and me both out of our misery."

Inside, I groaned. She was right. It was better to end the torment than to run through an endless scroll of whys and how comes. I flipped over the letter and thumbed the wax seal with the Hendricks family crest. My hands trembled as I opened the envelope. Removing the papers within, I unfolded the first, which appeared to be a letter. I scanned the words on the page, seeking understanding to my questions, but the jumble of letters meant nothing to me, and I held the pages out to Pippa. "Can you read it, please."

She took the pages, and I settled back in my chair, pulling the quilt tighter around me to still the vibrations chattering my teeth as nerves coursed through me.

Pippa's soft voice filled the room.

My dearest friend,

Something has come up that required I take my leave of London early. I know I promised to return one last time before my departure. Please know that I did not fall into my behaviors of the past and this time there is a purpose beyond my actions. Enclosed is the information to a trust account I've set up to care for you and Callie. It is the least I could do for you both. I know you see my existence in her life as a bad thing. That I will only cause her pain, and maybe so, but I will do everything within my abilities to make it not so. I hope to prove to you that I am worthy of your friendship and our daughter. Upon my return, in the spring, we'll sort out where we go from here. Until then, please be well and send my regards to the child and Miss Philippa.

> *Sincerely, your friend,*
> *Charles*

Tears pooled in Pippa's eyes as she dropped her hand with the letter to her lap.

I lifted a hand to brush away the tears cascading down my cheeks. "It wasn't as I feared. He promised to return."

"And I believe he will. Fate has smiled on you, my friend. The future doesn't seem so dismal anymore. Callie will be cared for, and she will know her father—even if she doesn't know of her birth tie to him, she will know him—and you will have your friendship."

"That is more than I could have hoped for."

Pippa clasped the letter to her heart. "My heart swells for you all."

A smile touched my lips and hope for the future surged within me.

Epilogue

Charles
Livingston Plantation

THE ENCLOSED CARRIAGE TURNED UP THE LANE TO Livingston and a familiar sadness expanded in my chest with the flood of memories—how Olivia would race out of the main house to greet me, breathless, with a beautiful warm smile, often with Willow in her arms or stationed at her side.

The carriage came to a stop at the carriage stone, and the footman hurried to open the door. I tucked the book I'd purchased for Willow under my arm and reached for the pup.

"Papa!" The small squeak tugged at my heart as I disembarked.

Willow, adorned in a pale blue muslin dress with a white pinafore, bounded down the front steps. Her dark ringlets bounced and her green eyes were alive with excitement. I removed my hat and dropped to my knees as she launched herself into my arms. "Oh, Papa—you're home!"

I kissed the top of my nine-year-old's head, choking back tears at her gleeful embrace. I'd missed her.

She pulled back at the sound of the pup's displeasure at being squished. Her eyes grew huge. "You brought me a dog!"

"Now why would I do that?" I grinned at her.

Her eyes narrowed. "Because you always must bring me something, because it means you are thinking of me." She reached for the pup.

"Is that so?" I said, releasing the critter into her eager hands.

The pup tugged at a ringlet of her hair and whipped his head side to side, releasing a low growl. Willow giggled with delight.

"His name is Beau," I said, rising to my feet—already forgotten.

She cocked an eye at me. "You named him already?"

"Yes, I suppose I have." I read the questioning in her eyes, but her excitement dismissed it for the time being. She caught sight of the book under my arm.

"And a book, too!"

I removed the book and handed it to her. She gave the pup to Mary Grace, who always seemed to be in Willow's shadow. The slave child gripped the dog pushed at her, not sure what to do, and stood holding him awkwardly away from her body.

Willow caressed the cover of the book with appreciation. "You must read it to me, Papa. Straightaway." She slipped her hand into mine. "Shall I ask Mammy to prepare you a bath?"

"Welcome home, Masa Hendricks." Mammy met us on the veranda. "De li'l missus has been awfully excited for your arrival."

"I can see that." I smiled down into Willow's upturned face.

For the moment she'd be happy, and I'd spend every moment that evening playing puppet to the spoiled girl's whims. I didn't look forward to the tantrum that would follow when in the morning I'd inform her that I'd be leaving again. A matter of great importance required my dedication—the human cargo hidden in my warehouses, awaiting shipping to my estate in Rhode Island.

If you have enjoyed my work, please leave a review on Goodreads, or the platform you purchased the books from. Your reviews are crucial in spreading the word about my books, and I am sincerely grateful for this support from readers.

THE PROMISE BETWEEN US

NOVELLA THREE

ABOUT
the Author

Naomi is a bestselling and award-winning author living in Northern Alberta. She loves to travel and her suitcase is always on standby awaiting her next adventure. Naomi's affinity for the Deep South and its history was cultivated during her childhood living in a Tennessee plantation house with six sisters. Her fascination with history and the resiliency of the human spirit to overcome obstacles are major inspirations for her writing and she is passionately devoted to creativity. In addition to writing fiction, her interests include interior design, cooking new recipes, and hosting dinner parties. Naomi is married to her high school sweetheart and she has two teenage children and a dog named Egypt.

Sign up for my newsletter: authornaomifinley.com/contact